Gerald

Encapsulated PostScript

Encapsulated PostScript

Application Guide for the Macintosh and PCs

Peter Vollenweider

Manager User Services
University of Zürich

Carl Hanser Verlag

Prentice Hall

First published in German 1989
by Carl Hanser Verlag
under the title *EPS-Handbuch: Encapsulated PostScript*

First published in English 1990 by
Prentice Hall International (UK) Ltd
66 Wood Lane End, Hemel Hempstead
Hertfordshire HP2 4RG
A division of
Simon & Schuster International Group

The Sonata clef design on the cover shows the mixing of
randomly placed Sonata font types, smoothed curves and
patterns; courtesy of John F. Sherman, ND Design Program,
University of Notre Dame, Indiana 46556, USA.

Printed and bound in Great Britain by
Dotesios Printers Ltd, Trowbridge, Wiltshire.

Library of Congress Cataloging-in-Publication Data

Vollenweider, Peter.
  (Encapsulated PostScript. English)
  Encapsulated PostScript : application guide for the
Macintosh and PC's / Peter Vollenweider.
     p. cm.
  Includes bibliographical references.
  ISBN 0-13-275843-1
  1. PostScript (Computer program language) I. Title.
  QA76.73.P67V65 1990
  005.265–dc20
                                              90-35469
                                                  CIP

British Library Cataloguing-in-Publication Data

Vollenweider, Peter
  Encapsulated PostScript : application guide for the
  Macintosh and PC's.
  1. Microcomputer systems. Software packages
  I. Title
  005.36

  ISBN 0-13-275843-1

1 2 3 4 5 94 93 92 91 90

Contents

Figures

Preface

The topic of this book is the application of Encapsulated PostScript (EPS) by Macintosh and IBM PC users. It addresses the Desktop Publishing user and the computer science student by introducing the Encapsulated PostScript File (EPSF) format. In Chapter 2, *Short Introduction to PostScript,* the reader gets a basic insight into the language, and the book also presents some PostScript examples, two in color. Chapter 4, *Mixing PostScript Files* forms the core of the book: it describes how text, graphics, and images may be mixed at the PostScript level. In order to mix PostScript files from various sources, the Encapsulated PostScript format serves as an interchange standard: EPS files may be imported, e.g. by Aldus PageMaker, Xerox Ventura Publisher, or MS Word. The major advantage to EPS files is that applications can import complex PostScript language-encoded illustrations for printing without having to provide sophisticated graphics support.

The construction of the SWITCH logo is developed in five steps in Chapter 5, the five programs are supplemented by structuring comments. In addition, some Macintosh and PC programs which are producing the EPS code, are introduced: Adobe Illustrator, GEM Artline, Corel Draw, Harvard Graphics, SmartArt, MC/PC View, and others. In Chapter 11, the latest version of Adobe's EPSF specification is presented.

The chronological order of PostScript development is as follows:

1976	Development of the interpretive language 'Design System' at the *Evans & Sutherland Computer Corporation* for computer aided design applications. Resemblance to the FORTH programming language.
1978	Development of the language 'JaM' at Xerox for VLSI design and graphics. Development of Interpress, the Xerox printing protocol.
1982	Adobe Systems Inc. is founded. Third implementation of the language, called PostScript, as an interpretive graphics language, describing two-dimensional printed pages. The interpreter resides in controllers for raster printers.
1987	The three companies Altsys, Aldus, and Adobe define the Encapsulated PostScript (EPS) file format.

IBM adopts and supports PostScript.

1988   Adobe presents the screen version of PostScript, Display
                            PostScript, and Color PostScript.

PostScript® is a registered trademark of *Adobe Systems Incorporated.*

Other books on PostScript

This book is unique in that it concentrates on the mixing of PostScript files and the
PostScript-related Macintosh and PC programs. References to the personal computer are
especially pertinent since a Mac-like range of applications is now available for the IBM
PC: e.g. PageMaker, MS Word, the graphics programs called Micrografx Designer and
Corel Draw under Windows, GEM Artline, or Harvard Graphics. Chapters and sections
on the following are particularly topical:

- Encapsulated PostScript Files (EPSF)
- Color Support with setcmykcolor (Chapter 3)
- The Macintosh applications Adobe Type Manager (ATM) and the Art Importer by
  Altsys (in Chapter 7)
- EPS Effects by Emerald City Software – now Adobe Systems: SmartArt and
  TypeAlign (in Chapter 4)
- EPSF Specification by Adobe, version 2.0

My previous book (published by Carl Hanser in 1988) presents a collection of 'real life'
PostScript examples. My favorite books are *PostScript Language, Program Design*
(green book), Adobe Systems Inc. (1988)[3], and *Real World PostScript*, Roth, Stephen
F. (1988)[16].

Thanks

Special thanks are due to my family and to Kurt Bauknecht, Teddy and Coni at the Computing Center of the University of Zurich who gave me sufficient time to research and
write this book. Technical support, mainly in the form of (Encapsulated) PostScript files,
was provided by the following persons:

- Many computer users and computer science students at the University of Zurich,
  Switzerland
- *Thomas Guggi,* UPCO Computer Systems, Zürich, Switzerland
- *Jean-Pierre Kousz,* K+K Computertraining, Wallisellen-Zürich, Switzerland
- *Ludwig Böckh,* IBM Labs, Böblingen-Stuttgart, Germany

- *Olaf Pluta,* Ruhr University Bochum, Germany
- *Corien Niezing,* Adobe Systems Europe, Amsterdam, The Netherlands
- *John F. Sherman,* University of Notre Dame, Indiana, USA
  (many thanks for the LearnPS cards, John)
- *Jim Von Ehr* and *Earl Allen,* Altsys Corporation, Plano, Texas, USA
- *James W. Rafferty,* Cricket Software Inc., Malvern, Pennsylvania, USA
  (now Creative Circuit Corp.)

Adobe Systems Inc., Mountain View CA and Amsterdam NL, gave permission for the EPSF specification to be included in this book (Chapter 11).

1.

PostScript — A Publishing Standard

PostScript as a page description language

PostScript (from *Adobe Systems)* is an interpreted, stack-oriented language for describing, in a device-independent fashion, the way in which pages can be composed of characters, shapes, and digitized images in black and white, gray scale, or color. Concerning the text/graphics field, PostScript is now the most widely used printer controller in the industry. It gives computer users total control over text, graphics, color-separations, and halftones.

The page description language recognizes a page that is created by the user, as a unity and converts the elements of the page into control data for the output device. The printing engine receives the control data in its own format and resolution. The resolution of these control data amounts for instance to 300 dots per inch (dpi) on a page printer or 1000 dots per cm on a typesetter. Today, PostScript compatible imagesetters are sold by all manufacturers of typesetters.

PostScript language programs are used for communication between a software product (PageMaker for instance) and a printing system, and enable the user to mix text, graphics, and images from various sources.

Competitors

The competitors of PostScript are the Document Description Language (DDL), and mainly the new imaging models of Microsoft under OS/2, and that of Apple (QuickDraw).

DDL was two years behind the market leader and failed because of the adoption of PostScript by IBM. Today, even Hewlett-Packard – producer of the Laserjet – is using PostScript. However, Hewlett-Packard recommends PostScript usage only for the 'top end' of the applications, for instance, if typesetting is required.

Microsoft wants to make the Presentation Manager the standard imaging model for displays and printers under OS/2. Presentation Manager includes a device-independent graphics programming language called Graphics Programming Interface (GPI). A PC magazine mentioned this single-imaging model may threaten Adobe's page description language. The QMS PM-10 printer is equipped with the GPI language that is used by Presentation Manager applications in order to display graphics. However, a new driver for PostScript printers is included in OS/2 version 1.2.

Likewise, Apple doesn't want to become dependent upon Adobe Systems Inc. and extends its Color QuickDraw imaging model. The Macintosh system 7.0 contains outline fonts which are freely resizable. In this case, the PostScript printers would be needed only for some PostScript effects, for typesetting, and for the 1-MByte Macintosh that masters the old screen fonts only. In late summer 1989, Apple announced it would use the PostScript compatible interpreter from Microsoft for the LaserWriter, i.e. a Non-Adobe PostScript clone.

Seybold (Oct. 9, 1989) reported:

'In exchange for the font technology, Microsoft will license to Apple the PostScript clone technology it obtained when it acquired Bauer Technology earlier this spring. In fact, Microsoft now intends to move aggressively into the output imaging technology business. Apple and Microsoft will work to make the Microsoft PostScript with Apple Royal font technology (TrueType) the dominant form of PostScript. With input and suggestions from Apple, Microsoft intends to extend and enhance its PostScript implementation. By implication, this could well lead to two principal PostScript development centers – Adobe and Microsoft – each promoting a somewhat different form of PostScript.'

Imaging models and outline fonts in the nineties:

Competitors:	Apple	Adobe NeXT	Microsoft OS/2 PM	IBM OS/2 PM	Hewlett-Packard
Font format	TrueType	Adobe	TrueType	Adobe	Intelli-font
Imaging model		Display			
screen	QuickDraw	PostScript	GPI	GPI	GPI
printer	QuickDraw	PostScript	GPI	GPI	PCL 5
2nd language for printer	PostScript*	--	PostScript*	PostScript	PostScript

* Non-Adobe PostScript (Bauer)

TrueType = Royal

Some typical PostScript effects

- Cubic curves (Bézier curves) and random-generated cubic curves
- Any color (e.g. 33% blue)
- Continuous color from light to dark (fountain)
- Saving the gray scales and color scales of images and modifying the halftone screen
- Broken point sizes (e.g. 9 1/4 point)
- Threshing and scaling types
- Rotating and/or slanting text and graphical objects
- Filling types with shadow or pattern, see Figure 1.
- Any line width of character outlines

A letter is treated as a graphical object and may undergo any graphical modification.

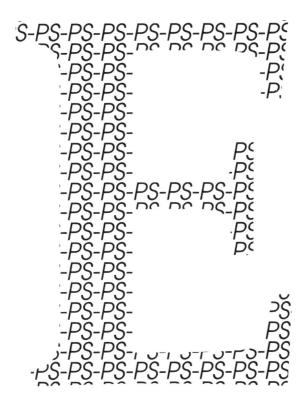

Figure 1   A PostScript effect

Spotlight: Encapsulated PostScript (EPS) files

In order to allow the inclusion of text, graphics, and images from various sources, the EPS File format was defined by the three companies Aldus, Altsys, and Adobe. Encapsulated PostScript (EPS) files are always complete. There is no need of any further printer initializations, nor of downloading any prep files or additional PostScript prologues.

In order to support the WYSIWYG principle (What You See Is What You Get), the PostScript file may be supplemented optionally by a bit-mapped screen representation. This means, that the importing or embedding application can display the document at the screen (preview facility) while using the PostScript program for printing or typesetting. This mechanism guarantees the high quality of the illustration, but enables the user to see and to scale an approximation at his or her screen.

The format of the screen representation:

Macintosh   PICT format (QuickDraw)

IBM PC   MS Windows MetaFile or TIFF (Tag Image File Format)

The well-known publishing programs capable of importing EPS files are Aldus Page-Maker, Xerox Ventura Publisher, MS Word, Word Perfect, MS PowerPoint, Quark XPress, and Ragtime from Germany. These support the WYSIWYG principle. The typical Macintosh user generates the EPS language code by using the FreeHand or Illustrator '88 tools. Finally, the EPS file will be embedded by the PageMaker program: FreeHand → EPSF → PageMaker. The IBM PC user will, on the other hand, generate the EPS language code by using Corel Draw: Corel Draw → EPSF → Ventura Publisher. A different IBM PC user may follow the route: Micrografx Designer → EPSF → MS Word.

See Chapter 4 'Mixing PostScript Files'.

The Adobe publication *Colophon* No. 5 recommended:

Prevent Headaches!
Use the remarkable EPSF!
to Import and Export PostScript Language Files.
Transport Text, Images, Graphics into or between applications.
Get both worlds:
Include a bit-mapped representation for screen previewing
and preserve the high quality of the original illustration for printing.

A user at North Carolina State University mailed the following statement to the Postscript forum: 'EPS is very little different from standard PostScript code. It has additional information embedded in comments at the top of the file that tell the program how big the graphic is, etc., and it has its origin set to the corner of the graphic, rather than the corner of the page. In Mac and IBM PC worlds, there are additional resources to allow the program to display a bitmapped equivalent to the PostScript. Other than that, it is plain vanilla PS code.'

IBM recovers lost ground

Three American companies — their names all begin with the letter 'A' — first made Desktop or Electronic Publishing popular:

- The *Apple* company put the user-friendly Macintosh computer onto the market.
- The *Aldus* company invented the layout or page make-up program called PageMaker.
- Based on a Xerox printing protocol, *Adobe Inc.* developed the PostScript page description language.

IBM has accepted the challenge. Since 1988, IBM has offered a system for electronic or desktop publishing. It consists of a Personal System/2, a color or monochrome screen, the IBM mouse, the IBM 4216 page printer, and the PostScript adapter board. With the help of PostScript, the output data of the PageMaker layout program are converted into control commands for printers and typesetters. Unlike other systems, the conversion doesn't occur inside the printer, but in an adapter board of the PS/2 or personal computer. This may be both an advantage (internal data communication at high speed) and a disadvantage (networking impossible).

The *Personal Page Printer II* supports parallel communication, AppleTalk, and serial RS232. It is network-capable and can cooperate with all computers, so with the IBM PC, PS/2 models, RT systems, and other computers including the Macintosh.

There also are low-cost solutions. An alternative is an IBM-compatible personal computer together with the *Xerox Ventura Publisher* or *MS Word* software. This configuration is supplemented by a PostScript-compatible page printer, for instance from NEC, QMS, Qume, Texas Instruments, or Fujitsu. A very low-cost solution is a LaserJet II printer upgraded by the PacificPage cartridge or a LaserJet III upgraded by the HP Printer Cartridge.

Let's follow a Laser Lovers discussion: 'Laser printer for IBM and MAC advise. Hi... I am looking for the same info as Felix but have the following question. Can the HP Laserjet II (with lots of RAM) and a PostScript emulation cartridge act like the Apple Laserwriter? Imran'

'Yes, for about $800, an HP LJ II with 2MByte RAM and, say, PacificPage would essentially have the Apple LaserWriter Plus functionality. In fact, Pacific Data also has a PS cartridge for the HP LJ IIP. Hewlett Packard is expected to release their IIP PS firmware any day, now. Alternatively, for approximately $270, you could purchase QMS's (Imagen) UltraScript PC Plus. This versatile software runs on MS-DOS or under Windows. It interprets PostScript on the PC or PS/2 and can output to a large variety of laser printers including HP LJ II and IIP, ... Ed Garay, University of Illinois at Chicago'

IBM will supply all its publishing printers (e.g. the IBM LaserPrinter, IBM 4019) with PostScript. For details of the PostScript interpreter on the IBM mainframe, see Chapter 10.

Types, typefonts, and typefaces

The PostScript font files are not labeled 'Encapsulated', because the above-mentioned three companies defined the EPS files for describing illustrations only.

The first generation of PostScript printers and the Linotype typesetter – at the beginning of 1987 – had built-in the following standard typefaces only: Times, Helvetica, Courier, and Symbol, where, for instance, Times consists of a roman, an italic, a bold, and a bold-italic font. 'Font' means all representative characters of one particular style of a typeface, e.g. roman or bold. However, the Apple LaserWriter Plus had built-in 37 fonts and the Agfa P400PS LED printer did 66 fonts. PC users enjoyed the facility choosing typefaces in any point size. This is supported by PostScript defining the fonts 'intelligently' as outline fonts, as opposed to bitmap fonts. Outline fonts are freely resizable.

You can distinguish between PostScript Type 1 and Type 3 fonts. The Adobe Type 1 fonts are encrypted – from the user viewpoint unfortunately! In addition, they have special hints for improving the resolution of small sizes of type. The font designer provides a set of instructions, known as hints, that will tell the computer how to modify character outlines so they fit the grid of dots. Before the other manufacturers had built such hints into their font descriptions the Adobe fonts were of better quality. However, other companies such as Autologic, Bitstream, Compugraphic, Linotype, and Monotype have now recovered the lost ground. An agreement between Adobe and Compugraphic, Monotype, and Varityper has enabled these companies to use Adobe's font technology. Publication of the Type 1 font format, scheduled for first quarter 1990, documents the encryption and hinting of fonts. It is this specification that Adobe has held as a trade secret.

Downloadable fonts

Many companies offer downloadable fonts. These fonts aren't built-in inside a printer, but must be downloaded as a PostScript language code into a page printer before usage. When the printer is turned off, the downloaded fonts are discarded except for those fonts saved on a built-in hard disk (Agfa, Linotype, Varityper, etc.). PostScript fonts are offered by:

- Adobe,
- Berthold,
- Bitstream,
- Casady & Greene,
- Compugraphic,
- Letraset,
- LetterPress,
- Linotype,
- Monotype,
- Varityper, and many others.

An example of a downloadable font is shown in Figure 2.

Total memory:
239616
Memory used:
156455
 Free memory:
83134

Figure 2   The Sonata font

Both the IBM PC and Macintosh users may select such fonts in any point size, where the resolution capability of the output device is always exploited to its maximum potential. This means you always achieve the highest possible printing quality.

The advantage of the Bitstream fonts is that they may be used on a PostScript device *and* a HP LaserJet printer. The numerous Bitstream fonts also operate on all PostScript-compatible typesetters such as Linotronic, Varityper, and Compugraphic. The Bitstream fonts are *not* encrypted, making the usage and operation easier.

Private users and some companies have developed and edit their own types on a personal computer by using the *Fontographer, TypeStyler, LetraStudio* programs (on Mac) or by *Publishers Typefoundry* or *Type Studio* (on IBM PC) and transfer the PostScript file onto a PostScript output device. See Chapter 7 'Constructing Your Own Characters'.

Screen fonts

The *screen fonts* are used for displaying the typefaces at the screen only; the true PostScript outline fonts which are freely resizable are used for printing. To date, all screen fonts have been coded in a bitmapped format and may be modified by a bitmap font editor. Screen fonts for IBM PC computers are provided in two formats: Adobe Binary Font (ABF) and Microsoft Windows (FON) format.

In September 89, *MACUSER* wrote: 'Since font outlines are so versatile, we should abandon bit maps and use outline fonts for both screen and print.' US MicroLabs markets *FontSizer,* a software that produces precisely sized bitmapped screen versions of any PostScript outline font in sizes from 12 to 127 points. Provided you have access to a PostScript printer, this scheme is inexpensive. True 'What You See Is What You Get' solutions are the Adobe Type Manager (ATM) and Apple's resizable outline fonts in the Macintosh System 7 (TrueType). Concerning the font description, ATM is a kind of Display PostScript.

PostScript-compatible devices

The page printer market is growing rapidly. While in the year 1988, 451,000 devices without or with PostScript were sold in Western Europe, the foreseen European market volume for the year 1992 will amount to some 4500 million dollars.

Manufacturers of PostScript-capable devices

(Summer 1989):

- Agfa-Gevaert
- Apple Computer
- AST Research Inc.
- Autologic (typesetters)
- Canon
- Compugraphic (typesetters)
- Data General
- Dataproducts
- Diconix
- Digital Equipment Corporation DEC (Print Server)
- Fujitsu
- GCC Technologies
- General Computer
- Gestetner Lasers
- Hewlett-Packard (Printer Cartridge, JetScript)
- IBM (Page Printer, Advanced Function Printing, AIX/Windows)
- Kyocera
- Laser Connection
- Laser Team
- Linotype (typesetters)
- Matsushita (non-roman printer)
- Monotype Lasercomp (typesetters)
- NBI
- NEC Information Systems (non-roman printer)
- NeXT (display)
- Olivetti
- Panasonic
- QMS (Color PostScript, DIN A3 size)
- Quadram
- Qume
- Ricoh
- Scangraphic (typesetters)
- Schlumberger (Color PostScript)

- Scitex (interpreter)
- Sun (Display PostScript clone)
- Tektronix (Color PostScript clone)
- Texas Instruments
- Unisys
- Varityper (typesetters)
- Wang

To date, the PostScript language has licensees in America, Australia, Europe, and Japan.

Page printers on your desk

A page printer heavily used by office staff should be placed near their work area. Between Spring 1985 and December 1988 for instance, the University of Zurich installed 180 Apple LaserWriter and other PS page printers in offices and remote buildings. These page printers are partly attached to small AppleTalk networks, and partly to the Uni Zurich Local Area Network (LAN) with thousands of access terminals (Localnet 2000). In the second case, the LaserWriter's are either attached to the local net Tbox directly or to a printer port of a display terminal or personal computer connected with the LAN. Four Apple LaserWriter's are supplied with coin slots for use by the public; these printers are mainly used by students.

> Attention: for practical reasons, a laser printer supplied with a magnetic card reader or a coin slot must be controlled by a single workstation.

For a company or an academic institute whose buildings are scattered over a wide area, the page printers of Apple, Qume, QMS, Texas Instruments, etc. allow distributed printing close to work areas.

With regard to the LaserWriter II, the models II NT and II NTX only are PostScript-capable. Apple has not supplied a low-cost model with PostScript. On the other hand, the Hewlett-Packard company offers the well-known LaserJet printer with PostScript: with the *HP Printer Cartridge*.

To date, there are dozens of PostScript page printer brands and PC adapter boards (see Chapter 10). In July 1989, Apple announced it was developing its own PostScript clone for the future LaserWriters. It will use the TrueType outline fonts. Apple said:

- NO to the Adobe fonts, but
- YES to the PostScript language and interpreter.

Typesetters and large page printers

Today all manufacturers of typesetters sell PostScript-compatible imagesetters, Compugraphic for instance offers the CG 9400 PS with a resolution of up to 2400 dpi.

With regard to the University of Zurich, this institute operates a Linotronic 100 with a Raster Image Processor (RIP = PostScript controller) and four large PostScript-compatible printers by Agfa and Dataproducts. The old Linotype RIP 1, having an AppleTalk and a serial interface, was connected to a LocalTalk net and the Localnet 2000 LAN, see Figure 3.

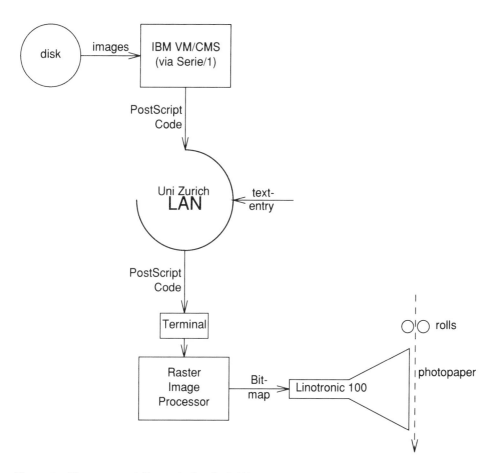

Figure 3   Typesetter serially attached to the LAN

The RIP model 2 and model 3 additionally have a parallel and Ethernet interface. There-fore, the RIP could also be attached to an IBM PS/2 or connected to a TCP/IP network.

The four page printers mentioned are not attached to the LAN, but directly to the mainframe. A Programmable Interface Translator (PIT) box handles the protocol conver-sion and the EBCDIC-to-ASCII translation. This box and other protocol converters are produced by the *INCAA* company in Apeldoorn, the Netherlands. Today, IBM has implemented the PostScript language interpreter on the mainframe under the VM/CMS and MVS operating systems, see Chapter 10.

Digital Equipment Corporation (DEC) offers a so-called Print Server: the PostScript-compatible LPS40 printer may be connected directly to a local network of the Ethernet and TCP/IP type and outputs up to 40 printed pages in the minute. Let's follow a Laser Lovers discussion: 'The LPS20 Laserprinter from DEC seems an interesting printer. According to its specification this printer has the following abilities: a) Postscript (300dpi) b) can print paper on both sides c) uses A4 AND A3 (size of two A4's) paper d) can be hooked up to DECnet and/or TCP/IP (network printer). Despite these nice fea-tures, I would like to get some extra information from people using this printer (and not from the people selling it). Regarding b) Is it possible to print both sides of an A3?'

'Yes. This printer can print duplex for all supported paper sizes (letter, legal, 10x14, 11x17, 12x17, 12x10 1/8, ledger, executive, half-letter, A3, A4, A5, B4, B5). ... John Gaffney by Adobe Systems Incorporated.'

While the *Agfa* printer (made in Europe) achieves a resolution of 400 dpi, the *Vari-typer* page printer prints on regular paper sheets with a resolution of 600 dpi. The A3 size is supported by Dataproducts, Fujitsu, QMS, and others.

Color printers

Since 1988, the QMS, Océ, and Tektronix companies offer PostScript compatible thermal-transfer color printers. The QMS *ColorScript 100* has an external PostScript controller and the thermal transfer color engine. The printer can save and output an A3-sized PostScript page in color. Tektronix sells the *Phaser* thermal color printer which can be attached to the Macintosh and the PC. The most important applications are the production of overhead slides and color proofing.

The companies Sharp, Colorocs Corp., and Kodak announced four-color laser print-ers. The availability of real color laser printers or ink jet printers is desirable because the consumables are much cheaper than with a thermal transfer printer.

The output of the thermal transfer printers and of other color printers may be used as color proofs, but unfortunately not as camera-ready copy. In order to produce colored publications in large quantity, printing houses use color separations. See Chapter 3 'Col-or Support'.

The color PostScript devices are supported by many applications: e.g. on the Macin-tosh by:

- Illustration graphics programs: Adobe Illustrator, FreeHand
- Layout programs: PageMaker, Quark XPress, RagTime, MS Word
- Presentation programs: MS PowerPoint, Persuasion, DeltaGraph, More II;

and on the IBM PC by:

- Illustration graphics programs: GEM Artline, Corel Draw, Illustrator PC, Micrografx Designer, Diagraph Windows
- Layout programs: PageMaker, Ventura Publisher, MS Word, Word Perfect
- Presentation programs: Xerox Presents, Mirage.

The application of color is particularly important in the area of *Desktop Presentation.*

Scanners

A scanner reads images, photographs and drawings into the computer. Many scanners can produce the EPS File format beside other formats (for instance the scanners of Agfa, Datacopy, IBM, and Sharp). A scanned image is coded hexadecimal, every 8 bits are represented as hex. XX, see Chapter 8.

Adobe evaluated the possibility of a participation with *Caere* in California in order to develop their own scanner that could generate the PostScript language code in the vector format (as opposed to the bitmap format). The solution would relate Caere's OCR technology with the 'auto trace' tool of Adobe Illustrator.

PostScript at the display

The Display PostScript system is an extension to the standard PostScript language interpreter originally developed for use on printers and typesetters. Now, printers and displays *could* have the same imaging model. The system allows the image on the screen to correspond to the text and graphics printed on a PostScript printer. Display PostScript offers the benefit of seeing on the screen exactly what will be printed later. IBM incorporated the Display PostScript system into its AIX operating system (UNIX).

The NeXT workstation (by Steve Jobs) included the Display PostScript system as an integral part of its operating system environment. The computer from NeXT was the first computer to use the Display PostScript imaging model. The NeXT Window Server is responsible for all the images that are 'drawn' on the screen. It has a built-in PostScript interpreter through which an application draws to the screen just as it does to the printer. As a result, the NeXT system delivers to the industry promise of true WYSIWYG. The display version of PostScript would also fit into other windowing systems, for instance *Microsoft Windows* or *X/Windows.*

The Sun stations are able to interpret the PostScript code directly and to output the document at the screen (under the NeWS windowing system); Sun developed a Display PostScript clone.

In October 1988, the MACWORLD magazine asked the president of Aldus, Paul Brainerd, the following question: 'Will you make a version of PageMaker that would work with PostScript as a display language?' His answer: 'Display PostScript is very important because it eliminates the difference between the screen and the printed result. In fact I think all of our customers would want Display PostScript if it were free. But, of course it's not free. If it were to cost $300 there would be wide acceptance of it as a display model; at $1500, it would probably interest only 15 percent of the people who use our products. If a third party were to implement a PostScript display controller board, we could quickly revise our software to take advantage of that.'

The Adobe Type Manager (ATM)

After Apple's announcement to supply QuickDraw with outline fonts, Adobe reacted by shipping the Type Manager. This software displays PostScript fonts at the Macintosh or OS/2 screen sharply and can output them onto non-PostScript printers. It is possible to scale the Adobe fonts to any size on your display and on non-PostScript printers. This means, one no longer needs to have many bit-mapped screen fonts.

The ATM package includes the outline fonts you need to generate high-quality type in various sizes and styles for Times, Helvetica, Courier, and Symbol typefaces. You can add more typefaces, including Kanji. The Hewlett-Packard DeskWriter is among the Non-PostScript printers the Adobe Type Manager works with. Enhancements in the ATM version 1.2 software include improved character spacing when printing from applications that don't support fractional widths (including MS Word 4.0 with the ImageWriter).

Emulating and cloning PostScript

When you have created or generated a PostScript file and saved it on disk, you can use any software emulator or emulator program.

GoScript by LaserGo is a DOS program to print PostScript files onto low-cost laser and matrix printers, e.g. HP LaserJet, Canon LBP-8, Epson, Toshiba, ProPrinter, NEC. It enables the user to output documents created by MS Word, PageMaker, or Ventura Publisher onto the LaserJet or a LaserJet-compatible printer. A German PC magazine titled in August 1989: 'PostScript for the Business Class: an Alternative to the 10,000-DM printer'.

A similar program is *Freedom of Press 2.0,* that gains in that it can output onto color printers. The *Kagema* company wrote: 'With Freedom of Press, you may print PostScript files onto non-PostScript color printers, such as HP-PaintJet or NEC P6. And even more: color information is rendered with corresponding gray scales, and Freedom of Press does make color separations on laser printers...' The version 2.2 of this emulation program supports the Adobe and Linotype fonts. The package contains 35 URW fonts;

in addition, PostScript Type 3 fonts (Bitstream, URW, LetterPress, etc.) and Type 1 fonts (Adobe, Linotype, Monotype, etc.) are supported by the new Freedom of Press version.

The *Ultrascript* PostScript emulation of QMS/Imagen runs on the Atari and the IBM PC. Ultrascript consists of two parts: the interpreter itself and a GEM user interface.

PostPrint by *Teletypesetting* is a PostScript emulator and – as the Freedom of Press competitor – can output PostScript files from the Macintosh onto printers such as HP LaserJet, DeskJet, and matrix printers, but also onto typesetters.

Generally, the software emulators run rather slowly.

PostScript interpreter

Generally, a PostScript interpreter consumes and processes the PostScript language programs; it resides inside either a printer or a workstation. A PostScript clone is an non-Adobe interpreter. There are more and more PostScript interpreters that don't come from Adobe.

Phoenix Technologies of Norwood, Massachusetts, developed *PhoenixPage,* a software package that not only provides a PostScript interpreter, but also handles such tasks as print spooling, queuing, networking, and other functions. PhoenixPage can be installed on any number of UNIX workstations to turn them into PostScript print servers.

LaserJet cartridge for PC users: when you plug a *PacificPage* cartridge into a LaserJet II, the printer is transformed into a PostScript printer. The brain of the cartridge is its PhoenixPage PostScript interpreter. In BYTE magazine in January 1990 titled *PostScript in the palm of your hand,* Howard Eglowstein wrote 'I recommend that anyone with a LaserJet and an occasional need for PostScript take a close look at PacificPage'.

The *Conographic* company produces a PostScript clone in the shape of a PC adapter card. The clone is called Conodesk 6000 and controls the low-cost Canon print engine.

Some clones can't cooperate with the licensed Adobe typefonts, as long as the Type 1 fonts are encrypted. Anyway, the use of downloadable fonts from Bitstream, Casady & Greene, etc. is possible without problems.

Books, reports, magazines ...

With the help of Adobe's page description language, various kinds of documents have been produced to date:

- Many books published in America and Europe since 1985, for instance a textbook on statistics (Oldenbourg, Munich), two books containing phonetical characters (Fretz, Zurich and Vita e Pensiero UCSC, Milan), a textbook on software technology (Carl Hanser, Munich), and this EPS book you are reading published by Prentice Hall, etc.
- Numerous reports and papers, for example a report of the Swiss department for foreign affairs.

- Countless presentation foils (overhead slides), and so on.
- In Sweden for example, all Volvo manuals are produced with the PostScript language.

With regard to the PostScript-capable printers and typesetters, images are partly generated synthetically from databases or information systems, and partly generated by scanners. The IBM scanner is capable of generating files in the *Encapsulated PostScript File* format.

The press in USA and Europe

PostScript helps in producing the master copies for printing magazines and newspapers. In America, much of the press has joined the PostScript language camp, for example the Senior Art Director for Technology of *The New York Times. Newsweek, The Wall Street Journal, The Washington Post* and *USA Today* also use the new technology. Karl Gude, Director of Graphics, The Associated Press, said: 'Adobe's PostScript software has brought high quality computer generated camera-ready artwork to the newspaper industry in a very cost-effective manner.'

In France, there is no newspaper with a circulation of more than 100,000 copies that doesn't employ PostScript in any form, primarily for graphics. An example is the Agence France Presse press agency producing up-to-date graphics and maps by Mac-Draw II and Adobe Illustrator. In the United Kingdom and France, the publishing program called *Quark XPress* which is used to make up a number of magazines into pages, e.g. *Science et Vie Micro, Profession Politique, Politis,* and the *Mineur de France* union magazine, is quite popular. Many English newspapers, such as *The Independent,* are using Macintosh computers.

Using PostScript at universities

The University of Zurich is one example only of an institution using the PostScript language as a standard. Not only academic institutes (e.g. University of Augsburg in Germany, Reading University in England, Lund in Sweden, Berne in Switzerland) – but also companies and other institutions may derive profit from implementing this language.

The computing center and the 'word processing' task force of the University of Zurich decided in 1985 to adopt the PostScript language as an output standard.

The computing center at the University of Zurich operates:

- Two mainframes (IBM and Hitachi) with the IBM VM/CMS and MVS operating systems with JES.
- Together with the Swiss Institute of Technology, the Zurich Academic Local Area Network with more than 8000 access points, see Figure 4. Most personal computers and terminals are connected to the broadband LAN by adapter T-boxes of the Localnet 2000 brand.
- A PC information center, a walk-in center, and a 'hot line' phone number for the PC users.

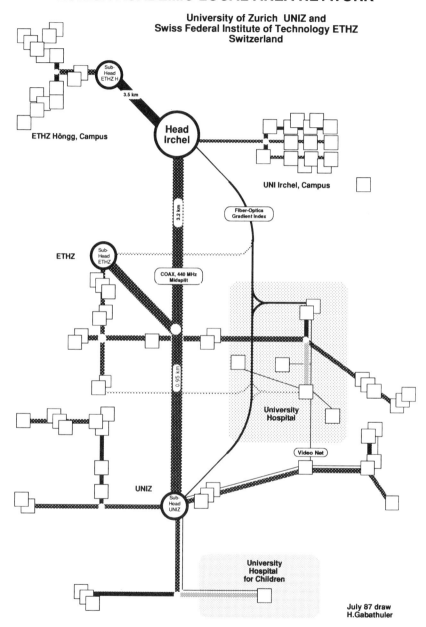

Figure 4   Zurich Academic Local Area Network (LAN)

The decision of the computing center proved correct; in 1985 however that decision was accompanied by uncertainty and risk.

Adobe advertises PostScript with the following statement (December 1988): 'The wide-spread confirmation of the PostScript language by producers, developers, and users made PostScript the final industry standard for page description languages.' While PostScript succeeded with the high-quality output devices, the competition to find the right imaging model for driving displays still goes on.

Electronic publishing software

A multitude of software components are used, not only at the University of Zurich, but also in many other places (e.g. Augsburg, Reading, Lund, Berne), for electronic or desk-top publishing. They are all able to generate the PostScript language code. Programs can be run on personal computers, workstations, midi computers, and mainframes.

Under UNIX	Framemaker of Frame Technology on the Sun stations, Technical Publishing Software of Interleaf; PrePress for color separations (OPI = Open Prepress Interface).
	NeXT station software such as WriteNow, TextArt and Top-Draw.
	Device independent Troff with tbl (for tables), eqn (mathematical equations), and pic (line graphics); the PostScript driver from Adobe is called Transcript.
Under VM/CMS	Knuth's T_EX of ArborText, Script with the Generalized Markup Language (GML).
Under MVS	DCF/Script from IBM; graphics packages Tellagraf and Disspla from Computer Associates, Statistical Analysis System SAS/GRAPH, see Figure 5.
	Troll from the Massachusetts Institute of Technology, National Algorithms Group NAG and Versaplot subroutine libraries.
PC software	MS Word, MS Chart, CA-CricketDraw, Aldus PageMaker, DesignStudio, RagTime, Adobe Illustrator, FreeHand, CA-Cricket Presents, Canvas, Adobe Photoshop, Fontographer, Mathematica (Wolfram Research), HyperCard, see Figure 6 (resolution 72 dots/inch).
	Under DOS also MS Word, Word Perfect, IBM PC Text4, Xerox Ventura Publisher, Aldus PageMaker, Troff, T_EX, Xerox Presents, MS Chart, Autocad, Lotus 123.

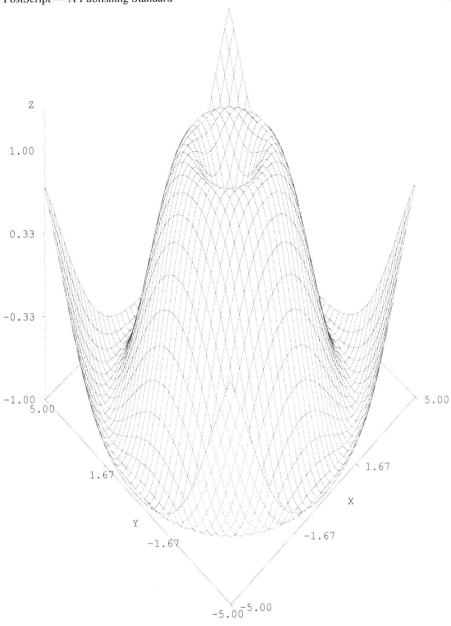

Figure 5   SAS/GRAPH: a cowboy hat

Figure 6   HyperCard: tiger

Drivers

Concerning the PC software, it is a fact that nearly any word processing, graphics, layout, or presentation program can generate the PostScript language code. This concerns both the Macintosh and the IBM PC platform. By using *DCA Image,* PC Text4 documents may be printed in the PostScript format. There are thousands of PostScript-compatible PC programs.

The users of the Advanced Function Printing (AFP) system have the option of printing their PostScript documents onto a range of IBM output devices under MVS and VM/CMS. This function is made available by a PostScript interpreter implemented on the IBM mainframe. IBM Manual: IBM Publishing Systems – PostScript Interpreter for Advanced Function Printing, Users Guide, SC34-5082-00, see Chapter 10.

IBM, SAS, and Computer Associates brought up the PostScript support for DCF/ Script, SAS/Graph, Tellagraf, and Disspla. Under VM/CMS, MVS, and DOS, the University of Zurich constructed print procedures, named PRINTDOC, to output ordinary text listings onto PostScript devices. Such conversion programs are offered by DEC and others.

Adobe offers the Transcript program for Troff and device independent Troff users under UNIX. Brian Bezanson of Adobe replied in the Laser Lovers list on the 'Sun386i → Laserwriter with/out Transcript?' subject:

'Transcript is designed as a set of translation filters from one format or another to PostScript. The enscript filter converts text files to PostScript and sends them to the printer. We also modify lpr to look at the file being printed, if it's ASCII, we do a simple translation to PostScript and then send the file to the printer, if it's a PostScript file – denoted by a '%!' as the first two characters of the first line, we send it down as straight PostScript. First, Adobe wrote Transcript and Sun is one OEM – you can call Adobe and get it for less (800/344-8335). You don't need Transcript to use a PostScript printer on a Unix machine if your applications create PostScript files and will send them to the printer, but if you need to print text files, Troff, Ditroff, Unix plot, Diablo 630, or Tektronix 4014 files, and don't have a conversion program – Transcript is really nice to have.'

The PostScript driver for T_EX is named *DVI2PS* and originates from Arbortext in Ann Arbor; the electronic mail address: BwB at Arbortext.Com. The drivers for the IBM mainframe may be copied over the European Academic and Research Network EARN/ Bitnet in Heidelberg Germany, the fileserver is LISTSERV at DHDURZ1. For IBM PC users, there is a driver from the University of Utah; the electronic mail address is Beebe at Science.Utah.edu.

What you see is what you get

The degree of 'easiness to learn to use' depends mainly on the software used. The user interface of the NeXT station, of the Macintosh and its programs (for instance Aldus PageMaker, Quark XPress, FreeHand), but also PageMaker, Corel Draw, and MS Word under MS Windows gain. The WYSIWYG principle applied for the most part (What You See Is What You Get) has proved to have some advantages over the abstract logic of the Troff, T_EX, and Script formatting programs.

Some graphics may be programmed by using the 'native' PostScript language – a fascinating but demanding and time consuming activity. The Chapter 2 of this book gives a basic insight into programming with the PostScript language. Some application programs offer a so called PostScript window, e.g. MS Word, Freehand, ReadySetGo, CA-CricketDraw, and Corel Draw. According to the application, the PostScript window is called the PostScript paragraph, PostScript fill pattern, PostScript text block, or similar. Inside this window, the user may specify his or her own PostScript commands or write small PostScript programs. It enables the user to perform special PostScript effects, e.g. altering a logo-type, creating new weights, expanding or condensing a type, making drop shadows. But the lion's share of the PostScript code is generated by the application automatically, i.e. by the driver. In most cases, the user need not be concerned with programming in PostScript.

The highest possible image fidelity between display and output is achieved by using Display PostScript, limited only by the resolution of the screen and the memory of the computer.

Benefits of using PostScript

The main benefit for the University of Zurich lies in having a universal output format which allows users to mix text, graphics, and images. Many other companies have standardized on the PostScript language, e.g. Volvo, Northern Telecom or Shearson Lehmann Hutton. The integration of text and graphics becomes a reality. For example: on a Macintosh or IBM PC, a line graphics figure is made with Adobe Illustrator or Corel Draw (see Chapter 6), then the PostScript file is transferred to the mainframe system. Now the figure can be embedded into a Script or Markup document − without cut and paste. Thus, PostScript is not only a page description language, but also serves as an interchange standard. Encapsulated PostScript (EPS) is particularly suited to interchanging, see Chapter 4 and Chapter 11. This style of document preparation combines the benefits of personal computers (user interface, graphical input) and the mainframe (disk space, databases).

In addition, graphics in the PostScript language format need less disk and memory space − in contrast to bitmapped and raster graphics − and do not stress the Uni Zurich LAN unduly. It is recommended several different output devices are used. A first draft may be produced on a small page printer connected to the LAN, a central LED printer may be used for producing the complete and final output. In order to produce high-quality publications, the computing center operates a typesetter (non-profit service) that outputs bromide paper, negative film or positive film.

Some companies plan to store documents, illustrations, and logos in databases. Many companies would be happy if they could access machine-readable versions of their logos, preferably in the Encapsulated PostScript File format and not just in the bitmap or raster format. A company logo stored in that way may be embedded into a PageMaker or Ventura Publisher document; but the logo might also adorn a letter written with the help of a word processing program such as MS Word or Word Perfect. Therefore, Encapsulated PostScript is also a format for describing and storing high-quality graphics and logos.

The following clip-art collections are published in the EPS File format:

- Collector's Edition I by *Adobe Systems*
- ClickArt by *T/Maker* (for NeXT)
- Digit-Art by *LetterPress*
- Images with Impact! by *3G Graphics*
- Cliptures by *Dream Maker*
- Works of Art by *Springboard Software*
- ArtClips by *Olduvai Corp.*
- Vivid Impressions by *Casady & Greene,* and many others.

Problems

It is often remarked that PostScript works too slowly. However, you must distinguish between text with many point sizes, text with one or two point sizes, and graphics and images. With regard to the rendering of images, the performance of the raster image processor (RIP) is improved with each revision. In the future, PostScript Level 2 will increase performance in several ways. 'Reduced Instruction Set Computer' (RISC) is the main way forward.

Adobe PostScript devices are expensive, this fact must not be hidden! Because each system contains a high-performance microprocessor to operate the interpreter and because Adobe earns licenses from every item sold, PostScript devices are in the top price bracket. However, Agfa-Compugraphic shows that the prices of the PostScript-compatible typesetters can come down. With regard to the high prices, there is another counter-argument: although it may be cheaper to buy a non-PostScript printer you may spend hundreds of additional dollars, installing all the required bitmap fonts.

Qume's *CrystalPrint Publisher* and Fortis *DP600P* are among the PostScript clones to deliver on the faster-but-cheaper basis. The internal instructions of a RISC processor are streamlined for improved performance. In 1990, the situation becomes even better. The LaserJet II printer upgraded by the PacificPage cartridge and the LaserJet III upgraded by the HP Printer Cartridge are very low-cost solutions.

Future

To conclude, the more PostScript is used in the publishing world, the more important it becomes. IBM, having already established *de-facto* standards, is supporting Display PostScript and will supply all its publishing printers (e.g. the IBM LaserPrinter, IBM 4019) with PostScript and the Adobe font technology.

PostScript Level 2 is the first major new release of PostScript software since it was introduced over five years ago. Adobe developed PostScript Level 2 based on input from its customers. PostScript Level 2 contains a number of performance enhancements, is easier for software developers to use, and adds important new functionality. In addition to consolidating recent extensions to the PostScript language, PostScript Level 2 includes such new features as extended color support and support for forms and patterns.

Making slides

The bitmapping method for describing fonts is not yet satisfactory. It is desirable therefore that some producers should implement the Color PostScript language. Of the recorder manufacturers, the Agfa subsidiary *Matrix* (ProColor, SlideWriter, PCR, QCR) signed a licensing agreement with Adobe. The RIP comes standard with AppleTalk, Centronics parallel and RS232 connectors, and 73 Adobe PostScript fonts. Concerning the other film recorders, PostScript implementation is a question of licensing. The prices of the devices with a PostScript controller will rise, however.

The use of the *Freedom of Press, MacRIP,* or *RIP-It* emulator is a low-cost alternative to the PostScript RIP (Raster Image Processor) solution.

High-resolution fax

To date, the resolution of fax transmission is low, resulting in quite mediocre copies. *GammaLink* introduces the first PostScript support for PC-to-fax transmissions, called GammaScript. This program allows GammaFax users to create presentation quality faxes using the thousands of application programs that support the PostScript page description language. The GammaScript software takes the output from any program that supports PostScript and translates it into a fax format file, with the help of the PostScript interpreter licensed from QMS.

Also Adobe is working on a high-resolution fax technology.

Japanese, Chinese, etc.

In order to support character sets such as Kanji, Adobe extended the PostScript language to provide two additional features: the ability to specify two sets of character metrics (writing directions) for a character, and the ability to build hierarchical composite fonts from normal (base) fonts. The font dictionary is extended by the *WMode* (Writing Mode) key: for most fonts a value of *0* indicates a horizontal writing mode (from left to right), and *1* indicates a vertical writing mode. In addition, a *Composite Font* is a collection of base fonts which are organized in a hierarchical fashion. Composite fonts support character sets with thousands of graphical symbols.

The LaserWriter II NTX-A or NTX-J contains a large number of Chinese fonts.

Display PostScript

Adobe tried hard to gain important manufacturers for Display PostScript. DEC, NeXT (Steve Jobs), and IBM decided in favor of Display PostScript, but Apple and Microsoft against! IBM incorporated Display PostScript in the AIX UNIX system, AIX/Windows and Nextstep. The system allows the image on the screen to correspond to the text and graphics printed on a PostScript printer.

UNIX: the Open System Foundation decided to develop a Unix on the basis of MACH, the Unix version of the NeXT computer. Now the 'battle' is being fought over the right single-imaging model for displays *and* printers.

In the future, Apple will push the QuickDraw imaging model with the TrueType outline fonts. But the Macintosh user still has the opportunity to use the *Adobe Type Manager (ATM)* that represents some kind of Display PostScript (at least concerning the font description). On other platforms, Display PostScript is operational. Sun was the first developer to implement a Display PostScript clone.

2.

Short Introduction to PostScript

The page description language serves as an interface between an application program and a printing subsystem. Normally, the PostScript language code is generated by a driver program, e.g. by the Presentation Manager, MS Windows, Adobe Illustrator, PageMaker, Xerox Ventura Publisher, or GEM Artline. However, PostScript can be generated by the end-user as well as a piece of a Lisp or C program.

Short comparison between PostScript and C

Let's take the first program from the C book by Kernighan and Ritchie:

```
main()
{
    printf("hello, world\n");
}
```

This program prints the character string

```
hello, world
```

and makes a final line feed to the beginning of the next line. When you try to translate this program into PostScript, it may look as follows:

```
%!
/Courier findfont 10 scalefont setfont
    0 100 moveto
    (hello, world) show
    0 88 moveto
showpage
```

At first glance, you cannot find much similarity between the two. This is because PostScript is a graphical programming language. You have to specify how the character string will be printed:

1. In which typeface *(Courier)*.
2. In which point size *(10)*.
3. At which starting position or coordinate point respectively *(0 100 moveto* means move 0 points to the right and 100 points up from the lower left corner of the paper sheet).

In addition, we program the line feed *(\n)* by doing a vertical motion downwards *(0 88 moveto)*.

Before printing the character string, we could assign it to a string variable:

```
/charstring (hello, world) def
charstring show
```

The stack: last in, first out

In the command line

```
1 0 0 setrgbcolor
```

setrgbcolor is the operator, while the operands consist of the three numbers. The *setrgbcolor* operator sets the current color parameter in the graphics state to a color described by the operands *red, green,* and *blue,* each of which must be a number in the range 0 to 1. The example establishes the red color used subsequently to paint shapes such as lines, areas, and characters on the current page.

PostScript is a stack-oriented programming language. The stack is a storage area available to a program in order to store objects temporarily. The PostScript operators take their operands from the stack and put the results in the stack as well. The LIFO principle (Last In, First Out) is valid. The object pushed to last in the stack, is popped out first.

PostScript uses the postfix notation. For instance:

```
10 10 moveto
```

The two operands stay at the left hand side of the operator.

```
10 10 moveto 100 100 lineto
```

is equivalent to:

```
100 100 10 10 moveto lineto
```

The *moveto* operator takes the two *10's,* because these are pushed onto the stack last.

10 means 10 typographical points = 10/72 inch. *10 10 moveto* makes a movement to the position (10,10) in the coordinate system. The origin of the coordinate system is placed at the lower left corner of the paper sheet. With *100 100 lineto* we are defining a line from the current position (10,10) to the new position (100,100).

By doing this, you have not yet drawn a stroke, merely constructed a path.

The LearnPS tutorial by John F. Sherman, shown in Figure 7, gives some moveto examples:

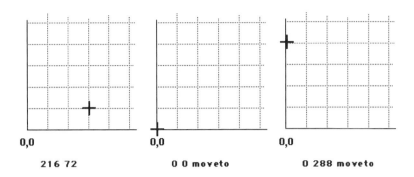

Figure 7   LearnPS moveto examples

Calculating and counting with PostScript

```
70 90 add 2 div
```

gives

$$\frac{(70 + 90)}{2} = 80.$$

For the computation of the arithmetic mean, you could define an equation:

```
/mean { add 2 div } def
```

Now, the equation is called up by saying:

```
70 90 mean
```

The PostScript interpreter puts the resulting 80 onto the stack.

Variables also may be defined:

```
/x 100 def
```

Now, you may increment the value of the *x* variable by 1:

```
/x x 1 add def
```

In the following example, we use the *number* variable as a counter. Each time the counter reaches 5, we are performing a certain action *(show)* and reset the counter to zero.

```
/number 0 def            % counter
/@m { moveto
   /number number 1 add def
   number 5 ge           % greater/equal to 5 ?
   {gsave
       (XXX) show
       /number 0 def
    grestore} if
   } def
```

ge (greater or equal) is a relational operator. Similar operators are *eq* (equal), *ne* (not equal), *gt* (greater than), *le* (less or equal), *lt* (less than), and so on.

In the example, the *@m* routine is defined. Such a routine may be used by a driver program to enumerate each fifth output line of a book text, see Figure 8.

Manipulating the stack

Most PostScript programs use operators to manipulate the stack. The *dup* operator duplicates the top-most object. The *exch* operator interchanges two objects, i.e. the two upper objects. The *pop* operator takes an object from the stack and discards it. Summary:

dup	duplicates top element
exch	exchanges top two elements
pop	discards top element
copy	duplicates top n elements
index	duplicates arbitrary element
roll	rolls n elements
clear	discards all elements
count	counts elements on stack
mark	pushes a mark onto the stack

What Is Electronic Mail?

Subject: Wanted: Help with apples and
nuts.

A month or so ago, a program was
5   posted to the net to convert a number of
apples into a number of nuts.
Unfortunately, my computer couldn't
find the result. After a fair amount of
hacking, I found (empirically) the
10   appropriate conversion factor between
the apples and the nuts. This took a bit of
black magic and the sacrifice of a
reasonably large amount of paper. I also
modified the program to (a) create
15   (scaleable) nuts (b) take these nuts and
produce more on demand. This (almost)
worked correctly. My one remaining
problem is that, since the program appear
use the relative positioning method, the
20   program needs to know about apple
weight information...

Has anyone out there done this
already and have any pointers on this?
Thanks in advance. Bill Winterfeld.

Figure 8   Numbering text lines

Equation for computation of the tangents:

```
/tan { dup sin exch cos div } def
```

Let's invoke this equation:

```
30 tan   % calling
```

1.   The operand first is duplicated: 30 30.
2.   The *sin* operand takes the upper 30 and gives back 0.5 as the result. Current state of the stack: 30 0.5.
3.   *exch* interchanges the two objects: 0.5 30.
4.   Now, the *cos* operator is in action, resulting in the following contents of the stack: 0.5 0.866.
5.   Finally, the *div* operator divides 0.5 by 0.866:

$$\frac{0.5}{0.866} = 0.577$$

As the final result, the stack contains the 0.577 value.

Flow control and loops

The PostScript language offers some operators to control the program flow, for instance *if, ifelse, for, repeat, loop, forall.*

The *if* operator executes something conditionally, dependent upon the value of a comparison.

```
/product load (Linotype) eq
                { ..... } if
```

This example checks whether the output device is a Linotype typesetter or not. The *load* operator searches the dictionary for the *product* key and returns the associated value.

The *ifelse* operator is an extension of *if:*

```
number 5 ge
{... Code A ...} {... Code B ...}
ifelse
```

If the condition holds true (number >= 5) the Code A is executed, otherwise Code B is executed.

In the program loop

```
1 1 7 { ... corpus delicti ... } for
```

the 'corpus delicti' is executed seven times. The *for* operator presents a value at each pass of the loop, in the example 1 to 7 incremented by 1. The meaning of the operands of the *for* operator:

```
1               % starting counter value
1               % increment
7               % end value of counter
{ ... } for
```

Even simpler is *repeat:*

```
5 { ... corpus delicti ... } repeat
```

The PostScript code between the braces is executed five times. (See the example in Chapter 3 'Color Support')

The *forall* operator enumerates all elements of an array:

```
vektor
{   ...    }
forall
```

The number of elements of *vektor* determines how many times the code between the braces is executed. In the following example, you initialize the array with four elements:

```
/vektor 4 array def
836 7117 919 257 vektor astore
```

Often used PostScript operators

Before text can be printed the typefont and the point size must be known. For that, you are using the *findfont scalefont setfont* sequence. Example:

```
/Times-Roman findfont 24 scalefont setfont
```

We choose the regular Times font in the 24 point size. Here, size means the height of the typeface body (body is the old term). The LearnPS tutorial by John F. Sherman clarifies point size terminology, see Figure 9. Most PostScript typefonts have characters of proportional width. Only the Courier, Letter Gothic, and other typewriter fonts have equal-width characters.

The *show* operator prints character strings or words in the current font selected by the *setfont* operator. The current position is shifted to the right according to the character output.

```
144 144 moveto
(Type) show
```

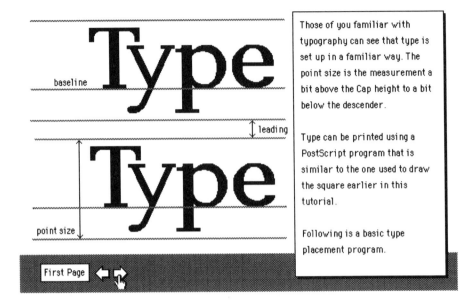

Figure 9   Point size (by LearnPS)

The *widthshow* operator additionally does expand the spacing between the words. Many drivers use the *widthshow* operator to justify the right margin (fix page layout).

```
3 0 32 (space between word and word) widthshow
```

The number 32 holds for the blank character (ASCII blank), of which the width has to be enlarged by 3 points.

Finally, the *showpage* operator outputs the current page by as many copies as the *#copies* variable specifies:

```
/#copies 3 def
showpage
```

You bracket (encapsulate) a single program segment by issuing the *gsave – grestore* operator pair in order to avoid the unwanted impact of the script on other parts of the document. The *grestore* operator restores that graphics state (current position, color, font, line width, ...), which was valid at the time of the *gsave* call.

An exercise in word processing

How can numbers be printed ranged right? Although PostScript isn't a formatting program you can use the PostScript language to program some basic word processing functions.

In order to print a column of numbers ranged right, you must take the following steps:

- Convert the number into a character string *(cvs)*
  In order to print a numeric value, the value has to be converted into a character string. The *number* variable is numeric, while *str* is a string variable.

- Determine the width of the character string *(stringwidth)*
  The *stringwidth* operator returns two elements onto the stack, of which only the width interests you (the other element is discarded by the *pop* operator).

- Execute the movement to the left *(rmoveto)*
  The size of the movement to the left corresponds to the width of the string; this value, being still on the stack, is made negative so that the *rmoveto* operator effects a movement to the left. The *neg 0 rmoveto* code makes a relative motion going from the current position; the first operand gives the (horizontal) *x*-coordinate (in the example negative), the second operand does the (vertical) *y*-coordinate (in the example 0).

- Print the character string *(show)*
  The content of *str,* i.e. the number in the form of a string, is printed.

```
%!PS-Adobe
% small exercise for newcomers
%%DocumentFonts: Times-Roman
%%Title: exercise.ps

/Times-Roman findfont 32 scalefont setfont
100 100 translate
newpath 0 400 moveto      % position
```

```
/number 7 def              % counter
/str 5 string def          % character string
 7 {
   /number number 1 add def   % count
   0 -32 rmoveto           % new line
      gsave
      number str cvs       % convert number
      stringwidth pop      % width of string
         neg 0 rmoveto     % motion to the left
      str show             % print
      grestore
 } repeat                  % loop

   showpage

%%Trailer
```

If you write down this exercise and download the file onto a PostScript-compatible printer, the loop is called up seven times. The numbers '8' to '14' are printed one below the
other, where both the single-digit and the double-digit number are ranged right. See Figure 10.

Figure 10 The result of the exercise

Graphics state

One further remark on the usage of the gsave/grestore operator pair: if you do not encapsulate the cvs/show segment with *gsave* and *grestore,* the printed numbers will not be
arranged one below the other, but shifted to the right, see Figure 11. The reason is that
the gsave/grestore pair always resets the current position to the beginning of the output
line. The current position – as the current path, the current font, the current color, and so
on – belongs to the graphics state. The *gsave* operator saves the graphics state (path,
position, color, ...). The *grestore* operator restores the previously saved graphics state.

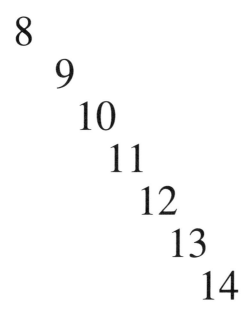

Figure 11   The result of the exercise without gsave/grestore

Don't be disturbed if you not yet know all operators used in the example, for instance
translate and others are discussed later.

The PostScript character set

The character set used in PostScript programs is the printable ASCII character set (96 characters), including the tabulator and newline characters:

```
!"#$%&'()*+,-./0123456789:;<=>?
@ABCDEFGHIJKLMNOPQRSTUVWXYZ[\]^_
`abcdefghijklmnopqrstuvwxyz{|}~
```

The % sign introduces a PostScript comment. All characters up to the line end are treated as comment and discarded by the PostScript interpreter.

Character strings have to be specified between parentheses:

```
(the quick brown fox)
```

The brackets mark an array, i.e. a one-dimensional matrix:

```
[ (United Kingdom) (Eire) ... (France) (Germany) ]
```

Procedures are specified between braces:

```
{ x0 neg y0 neg translate }
```

The *neg* operator multiplies its operand by -1.

Special characters – including the German 'umlauts' ä, ö, ü and the French symbols é, è, à, ç – are written as '\nnn'. Example André or Zürich:

```
(Andr\202) (Z\201rich)
```

The slash '/' has another meaning:

```
/Position { x0 neg y0 neg translate } def
```

The slash introduces a literal name. The interpreter does not yet execute *Position,* but pushes this object on the operand stack. The whole command line defines a procedure named *Position.* The procedure and its name are stored within a user dictionary in the printer memory and can be called upon any number of times in a PostScript program. Whenever *Position* is addressed, the operation between the braces is performed.

It is advisable to avoid using non-printable characters such as end-of-file (control-d) in a PostScript program.

The dictionary

PostScript offers the usual elements of a higher programming language, as data types (simple variables, arrays, strings) and control facilities (conditions, loops, procedures). Furthermore, PostScript supports associative tables, named dictionaries, allowing clear and error-free programming.

A dictionary is a table whose elements are pairs of PostScript objects (number, string, name, operator, ...). We call the first element of a pair the 'key' and the second element the 'value'. The language includes operators inserting a key-value pair into a dictionary, operators looking up a key and fetching the associated value, and so on. For instance, *put, get, load* belong to these operators:

put   associate a key with a value in the dictionary

get   get a value associated with a key in the dictionary

load   search dictionary stack for a key and return the associated value

length   number of key-value pairs in the dictionary

dict   create new dictionary

Usually, a key is the name of a variable or a procedure, for instance *Max* or *rectangle,* while the value consists of a number or a procedure body. However, a font dictionary associates the names of the characters with the procedures for drawing those character shapes.

When the interpreter seeks to execute a name object, it first searches for the key in the current dictionary. If the key isn't there, the interpreter searches the next lower dictionary on the dictionary stack. This continues until either it finds the key or it exhausts the dictionary stack. In the last case the interpreter issues an *undefined* error message.

Special dictionaries are *systemdict, userdict, statusdict,* and *errordict.* The *systemdict* dictionary is always the bottommost dictionary on the dictionary stack; it associates the names of all PostScript operators with their values (implementations).

When for instance you call the *quit* operator in *systemdict* the printer is restarted without out the need of manually powering it off and on again.

```
%!File: Reset.ps
systemdict begin quit
```

The *begin* operator pushes a dictionary onto the dictionary stack.

The *statusdict* dictionary is the repository for machine- and configuration-dependent operators and values in most implementations of the PostScript interpreter, for instance *setdostartpage, setpapertray.*

PostScript experts characterize the understanding of the dictionary philosophy as 'the royal road to PostScript mastery'.

Using dictionaries

This allows redefinition of any PostScript operator by using the user dictionary or your own dictionary. Example:

```
% userdict:
/showpage { } def       % dummying
    ...
```

If no dictionary is specified the interpreter puts the definitions into userdict.

```
% your own dictionary:
/mydict 11 dict def
mydict begin
    /bd { bind def } bind def
    ...
end
```

In order to build your own font you have to use a font dictionary:

```
% font dictionary:
/ExampleFont 12 dict def
ExampleFont begin
    /FontType 3 def       % your own font
    ...
    CharacterDefs ...     % definitions of types
    /BuildChar
      { ... } def         % mandatory
end
```

The error handling may also be redefined:

```
% errordict:
errordict begin
    /handleerror
      { ... } def
end
```

In the real world, not only is error handling redefined but also operators such as *copypage* and *erasepage*.

The PostScript program structure

The PostScript language standard does not specify the overall structure of a PostScript program. For a PostScript program that is a page description (i.e., a description of a *printable* document), it is advantageous to impose an overall program structure.

1. It is recommended that a page description consists of a prolog with the definitions and a script that describes the elements of the page.
2. A script of a multi-page document is organized as a sequence of independent single-page descriptions, bracketed by *save – restore* operators. These operators do save and restore the current state of the virtual memory in the printing system.

The occurrence of the character '%' signifies a comment. When the *showpage* operator is specified after the *restore* operator, *#copies* of the printed page are output.

```
%!PS-Adobe-1.0
%%Creator: Peter
%%Title: typesetter independent troff
%%Pages: 2
%%DocumentFonts: Helvetica Helvetica-Bold
%%BoundingBox: 0 0 612 792
%%EndComments
/#copies 1 def
    ... prologue ...
/m /moveto load def    % defining a motion
/s /show load def      % defining a string output
    ...

                       % defining ...

    ...
%%EndProlog

%%Page: 1 1
/saveobj save def
    ... page script ...
saveobj restore
showpage

%%Page: 2 2
/saveobj save def
    ... page script ...
saveobj restore
showpage
%%Trailer
```

The user coordinate system

The coordinate system of the PostScript user is determined by the horizontal x-axis and the vertical y-axis. The units are typographical points (approximately 1/72 inch); the influence of the graphics arts industry is apparent. Normally, the origin lies at the lower left corner of the paper sheet. The greater the x-value, the more to the right the position; the greater the y-value, the higher the position. The user may modify his coordinate system by issuing the *translate, scale,* and *rotate* operators.

The *translate, scale,* and *rotate* PostScript operators are based on the so-called Current Transformation Matrix (= CTM = current state). Now any required translation of the origin, a magnification, a reduction, or a rotation of the coordinate system can be achieved. The result is a new Current Transformation Matrix. Such a transformation may be applied to any graphical object, it is therefore well suited for a PostScript file to be embedded into a document (see next page).

The *translate* operator translates the origin of the coordinate system, and *scale* rescales the x- and y-axes of the coordinate system, see Figure 12.

```
0 0 translate    1 1 scale

160 0 translate    2 1 scale
```

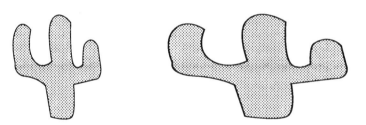

Figure 12 Playing with a cactus

Sections of a page can be geometrically transformed independently of each other.

Embedding a PostScript file

The following PostScript operators demonstrate the inclusion of a graphic, i.e. the importing of a PostScript file.

```
%!PS-Adobe
%%Title: Including
%%EndComments
% PostScript code of main document
   ...

save        % save state
%%BeginFile
    33 200 translate   % translate origin
     .7 .7 scale       % reduce size
    % PostScript code of the included graphics
      ...
      ...
      ...
%%EndFile
restore     % restore saved state

% the main document continues ...
   ...
%%Trailer
```

Because of the save/restore construct, the translation of the origin and the scaling are valid for the imported graphics only, not for the whole page or even the whole document. Without *save/restore* all following elements of the page would be moved to the right by 33 points and raised by 200 points, and the rest of the page or even of the document would be scaled down.

The *rotate* operator may be called up in three ways:

1. At the beginning of the PostScript file before the first page description. The consequence is that the whole document is rotated and printed landscape.
2. At the beginning of a page description. The consequence is that a whole page is rotated and printed landscape.
3. Inside the save/restore construct of an imported PostScript file. The consequence is that only the embedded graphic is rotated.

There is a similar situation when applying the *translate, scale*, and *clip* operators.

Setting characters and words

The *findfont* operator localizes the font dictionary containing the descriptions of the required Korinna typefaces. The slash identifies the font name. The *scalefont* operator sets the point size, i.e. the size of the letters. PostScript doesn't limit the point size, theoretically the font may be as big as Lake Geneva.

The *setfont* operator makes the specified font and size the current font and size.

The *show* operator prints letter by letter in the current font and size, see Figure 13. The PostScript programmer has to specify the letters to print between parentheses. If you don't want the letters black, or gray, but wish to stroke the type outlines only, then you have to issue:

```
(EPSF) true charpath stroke
```

instead of *(EPSF) show*.

The *showpage* operator at last outputs the printed paper sheet.

```
%!PS-Adobe
%%DocumentFonts: Korinna-Regular
%%Title: type.ps

/K /Korinna-Regular findfont def
%%EndProlog

100 100 translate
     20 rotate    % rotate the whole page by 20

K 72 scalefont setfont

% type setting:
72 216 moveto
0.9 setgray              % 10% gray
(EPSF) show

72 144 moveto
0.5 setgray              % 50% gray
(EPSF) show

72 72 moveto
0.2 setgray              % 80% gray
(EPSF) show

showpage
%%Trailer
```

The *%%DocumentFonts* information is useful to utility programs that may need to download special fonts to a PostScript printer before sending the document.

Figure 13   Setting the 'EPSF' characters

Line graphics with an ellipse

The most simple form of graphic is the line graphic. The elements of line graphics are lines and curves *(lineto, rlineto, arc, curveto)*. The lines may be stroked, dashed, or dotted. The curves are either a kind of spline (Bézier, cubic curves) or arc, see the LearnPS tutorial *arc example,* Figure 14.

The imaging model distinguishes two proceeding steps or levels respectively:

1.   Constructing a path (line, arc, etc.) with *newpath* and *lineto, arc...* . The maximum number of points specified in all active path descriptions is 1500. If the interpreter attempts to perform an operation that would exceed that limit, it executes the *limit-check* error.

2.   Stroking the path with *stroke*.

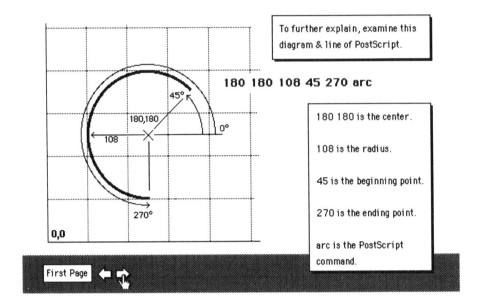

Figure 14 LearnPS arc example

The movements can be partitioned into the *moveto* and *rmoveto* operators. The difference lies in that *moveto* is based on absolute coordinates (distance measured from the origin), while *rmoveto* is based on relative coordinates (distance measured from the current position).

Note how the ellipse is defined *(xrad yrad scale* and *0 0 1 0 360 arc):* the routine makes a circle and scales the *x*-axis in a different way to the *y*-axis! The current transformation matrix is saved first *(currentmatrix)* and restored afterwards *(setmatrix)*. The *currentmatrix* operator fills the specified matrix with the current transformation matrix, while *setmatrix* replaces the current transformation matrix with the specified matrix.

A page can be represented by a set of procedures. And hence, libraries of procedures may facilitate construction of a compact page description.

The example here draws an ellipse with arrows, see Figure 15.

Note, where the *%%EndProlog* comment marks the end of the defining part and the beginning of the document script. The script addresses both plain PostScript operators and operators defined in the prologue.

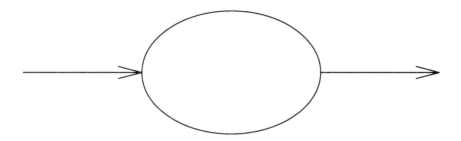

Figure 15 Ellipse with arrows

```
%!PS-Adobe-1.0
%%Creator: Andre and Peter
%%CreationDate: 5 Sept 1989
%%Title: line graphics with an ellipse
%%BoundingBox: 94 678 420 770
%%For: EPS Book
%%EndComments

/mtrx matrix def
/drawe                             % ellipse
{ /yrad exch def
  /xrad exch def
  /y exch def
  /x exch def
  newpath
  /savematrix mtrx currentmatrix def
  x y translate
  xrad yrad scale
  0 0 1 0 360 arc
  savematrix setmatrix
  stroke
} def
/dw { setlinewidth } def
/dn { newpath } def
/da { newpath arc stroke } def          % arc
/dc { newpath 0 360 arc stroke } def
/dr { rlineto } def                     % line
/ds { stroke } def
```

```
%%EndProlog
save
 .6 dw dn
94.4 723.7 moveto 92.6 0 dr 168.5 719.1 moveto
18.5 4.6 dr 168.5 728.3 moveto 18.5 -4.6 dr ds
256.4 723.7 69.4 46.2 drawe     % drawing ellipse
dn 325.8 723.7 moveto 92.6 0 dr 399.9 719.1 moveto
18.5 4.6 dr 399.9 728.3 moveto 18.5 -4.6 dr ds
restore

showpage
%%Trailer
```

Cubic curves or Bézier curves

As you know, quality graphics often contain cubic or Bézier curves. For constructing those, the use of the *curveto* or *rcurveto* PostScript operator is required. The LearnPS tutorial by John F. Sherman gives the *curveto* example as shown in Figure 16:

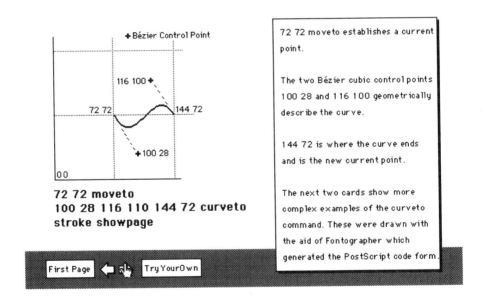

Figure 16 LearnPS curveto example

The syntax of *curveto* is:

```
x1 y1 x2 y2 x3 y3 curveto
```

Here, the segment going from the current position (X,Y) to the point (x3,y3) using the points (x1,y1) and (x2,y2) as the Bézier control points, is added to the current path. Having constructed the curve, the operator makes (x3,y3) become the new current point. The *rcurveto* operator functions similarly, however the points are not specified in absolute coordinates but in relative coordinates (relative to the current position):

```
dx1 dy1 dx2 dy2 dx3 dy3 rcurveto
```

The whole example consists of five varied paths, see Figure 17. Every path contains a straight line segment that in the first and second case flows into a cubic curve. The second path consists of three segments and has the following shape:

```
400 625 lineto
470.2 625    514 666 578 652 curveto
611.9 644.6 627 633 650 598 curveto
```

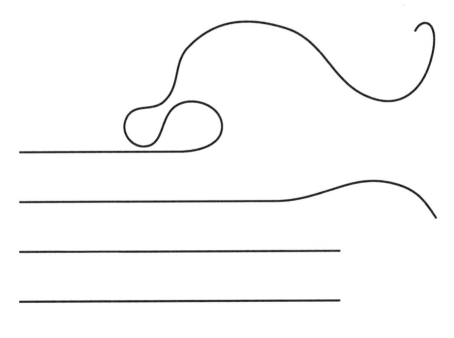

Figure 17 Cubic or Bézier curves

Here too, the two-level 'imaging model' is involved. After the paths are constructed they may be painted with black or gray ink by using the *stroke* operator.

An applied ink is opaque and overlays any object below it. All painting or inking operations are dependent on the graphics state: in the example, we are specifying a line width of 3 points and a color of 90% gray.

Remember that the percent sign (%) at the beginning of an input line introduces a PostScript comment that will be discarded by the PostScript interpreter.

```
%!PS-Adobe-1.0
%%Title: Cubic Curves
%%BoundingBox: 0 200 325 452
%%Creator: John F Sherman
%%CreationDate: 5 Sept 1989
%%EndComments

/cm {28.346456 mul} def
%%EndProlog

save
0.5 0.5 scale
3 setlinewidth    .1 setgray

0 700 moveto                % first path:
250 700 lineto
280 700 318.4 710.1 316 740 curveto
313.6 769.5 271.6 784.6 246 770 curveto
218 754 228 708 194 708 curveto
175.1 708 158 728 166 748 curveto
177.1 775.9 206.8 758.9 226 776 curveto
252.2 799.4 239.4 833 264 858 curveto
305.7 900.3 357.2 903.2 414 886 curveto
480 866 484 798 554 778 curveto
596.4 765.9 632 792 644 848 curveto
654.7 898.2 626 902 616 880 curveto
stroke
```

```
0 625 moveto                    % 2nd path:
400 625 lineto
470.2 625 514 666 578 652 curveto
611.9 644.6 627 633 650 598 curveto
stroke

% and the three last paths:
0 550 moveto 500 0 rlineto stroke
0 475 moveto 500 0 rlineto stroke
0 400 moveto 500 0 rlineto stroke

restore
showpage
%%Trailer
```

Note the *%%BoundingBox* comment. The bounding box encloses all the marks painted as a result of executing this program. All four values must be integers and represent the coordinates of the lower left and upper right corners of the bounding box in the default user coordinate system. Because of the *scale* operator, the lower left corner isn't located at the 0 400 position, but at 0 400/2, i.e. 0 200. The upper right corner of the bounding box is at the 324 452 position.

The BoundingBox information is of use to composition applications that incorporate this document into a larger one as an included illustration.

Virtual memory management

You noted the use of the *save – restore* operator pair. First, these operators encapsulate the graphics representation; any unwanted impact on other parts of the document is cancelled. Second, having executed the *restore* operator, the PostScript printer frees the memory area from occupation by the composite objects, the definitions, and the routines. The importing applications usually apply this method of memory management. It is a question of the virtual memory available in addition to the interpreter stacks and the 1-MByte page storage. The downloadable fonts too are stored in the virtual memory.

Various line widths

We begin by defining the *cm* variable for representing centimeters because the basic units in the coordinate system are typographical points (approximately 1/72 inch). The *rectangle* procedure may be self-explanatory: it builds the path for drawing a rectangle.

The line width may be set by the *setlinewidth* operator and modified by scaling the coordinate system *(scale)*. In the example, the line width of the innermost rectangle amounts to 1/10 cm; that's 1 millimeter. In the second pass through the loop the multiplication is 1/10 by 2 cm, in the third pass 1/10 by 3 cm, etc. All in all, the *for* loop is executed five times, see Figure 18.

In this example too, you are using the known *gsave grestore* operator pair inside the loop. As already mentioned – this operator pair saves and restores the graphics state. Without *gsave* and *grestore* you couldn't use the scale operator in that way since the magnifications would be added cumulatively.

```
%!PS-Adobe
%%Creator: Adobe Systems Inc.
%%EndComments

/cm {28.346456 mul} def        % centimeter

/rectangle                     % routine
  {newpath
    1. .666 moveto    -1. .666 lineto
    -1. -.666 lineto  1. -.666 lineto
  closepath
} def
%%EndProlog

gsave
10 cm 13 cm translate
1 10 div setlinewidth        % set to 1/10
1 1 5   % loop from 1 to 5
 {gsave
   cm dup scale    % multiply
   rectangle
   stroke
 grestore
 } for   % end of loop
grestore

% one additional call:
10 cm 5 cm translate
1 10 div setlinewidth        % set to 1/10
5 cm dup scale   % multiply
rectangle
stroke

showpage
%%Trailer
```

Figure 18   Setting and modifying the line width

A grid in centimeters

The grid is a special type of line art. A PostScript program such as *printgrid* makes visible the printing area of any printer on the paper sheet (e.g. A4 size). Note: since this book is smaller than A4, Figure 19 was scaled down.

Again, we begin by defining the *cm* variable for representing centimeters because the basic units in the coordinate system are typographical points (approximately 1/72 inch). *0 setlinewidth* means the lines are stroked in the smallest possible width (dependent upon the output device). The result looks quite good on the laser printer, but when outputing onto the typesetter, the line width may create surprise since such strokes are nearly invisible.

In the first program segment the centimeter grid is stroked, in the second program block the half-centimeter grid, and in the third program segment the millimeter grid.

The altogether six *for* loops are bracketed in each case by braces. The meaning of the operands of the *for* operator:

```
0  cm          % starting value
1  cm          % increment
20 cm          % end value
{ ... } for
```

For comparison in the C programming language:

```
for (i=0; i<=20; i++)     { ... };
```

In the first path through the first *for* loop, the following operators are executed:

```
0 cm -0.1 cm moveto
0 cm 27.1 cm lineto    % vertical stroke
```

In the last path through the second *for* loop, the following operators are performed:

```
-0.1 cm 27 cm moveto
20.1 cm 27 cm lineto  % horizontal stroke
```

Notice how the *setdash* operator defines the mm-dashes: always 1-mm dashes with 9 mm spacing.

```
[ 0.1 cm 0.9 cm ] 0 cm setdash % dashed
```

Here, the complete program example follows:

```
%!PS-Adobe-1.0 EPS
%%Title: grid.ps
%%BoundingBox: 0 0 595 839
%%DocumentFonts: Courier
%%Creator: Andre and Peter
%%CreationDate: 5 Sept 1989
%%For: EPS Book
%%EndComments

/printgrid {
/cm { 28.346456 mul } def
0 setlinewidth
/Courier findfont 10 scalefont setfont

newpath
   /str 2 string def
   /number 0 def
   0 cm 1 cm 20 cm {
      dup
      -0.1 cm moveto
      27.1 cm lineto          % vertical stroke
      number str cvs
      -6 3 rmoveto
      str show                % write down numbers
      /number number 1 add def
   } for    % end of loop

   /str 2 string def
   /number 0 def
   0 cm 1 cm 27 cm {
      dup
      -0.1 cm exch moveto
      20.1 cm exch lineto   % horizontal stroke
      number str cvs
      3 -3 rmoveto
      str show                % write down numbers
      /number number 1 add def
   } for    % end of loop

stroke

% end of first program segment drawing the cm strokes
```

Remember, the *dup* operator duplicates the top element on the operand stack, while the *exch* operator exchanges the top two elements.

```
newpath
    0.5 cm 1 cm 19.5 cm {
        dup
        0 cm moveto
        27 cm lineto              % vertical stroke
    } for    % end of loop

    0.5 cm 1 cm 26.5 cm {
        dup
        0 cm exch moveto
        20 cm exch lineto         % horizontal stroke
    } for    % end of loop

stroke

[ 0.1 cm 0.9 cm ] 0 cm setdash % dashed
newpath
    0.1 cm 0.1 cm 19.9 cm {
        dup
        -0.05 cm moveto
        27.05 cm lineto           % dashes
    } for    % end of loop

    0.1 cm 0.1 cm 27 cm {
        dup
        -0.05 cm exch moveto
        20.05 cm exch lineto    % dashes
    } for    % end of loop

stroke
} def
%%EndProlog

% calling printgrid:
printgrid showpage
%%Trailer
```

Regarding the display of the centimeters, you again had to convert the values into character strings *(number str cvs)*. The *number* variable is numeric, *str* is a string variable. Subsequently the *show* operator printed out the character string.

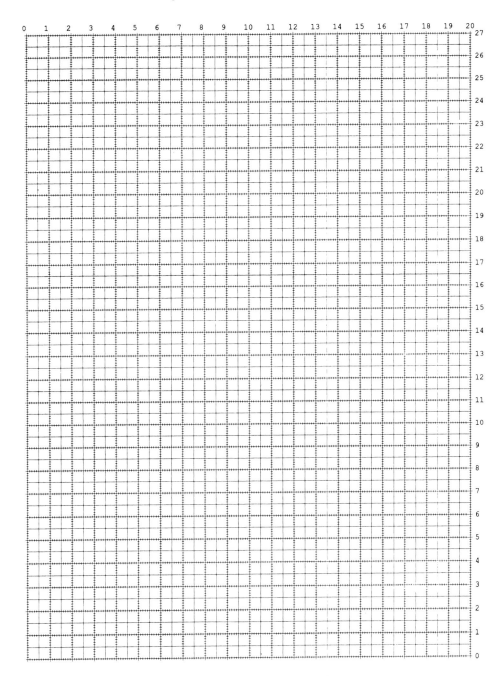

Figure 19 Grid in centimeters

3.

Color Support

PostScript-compatible color devices

As mentioned in Chapter 1 – the QMS and Tektronix companies offer PostScript compatible thermal transfer color printers. The QMS *ColorScript 100* has an external PostScript controller and the thermal transfer color engine. The printer can save and output an A3-sized PostScript page in color. Tektronix sells the *Phaser* thermal color printer, which can be attached to the Macintosh and the PC. The most important applications are the production of overhead projection originals and color proofing.

The companies Sharp, Colorocs Corp., and Kodak have announced four-color laser printers. There is a market for real color laser or ink jet printers, since the consumables are much cheaper than with the thermal transfer color printers. The first company to equip a film recorder with Color PostScript is *Matrix,* an Agfa-owned company.

Color PostScript devices are supported by many applications. E.g. on the Macintosh by:

- Illustrator and FreeHand
- PageMaker/PrePrint, MS Word, Quark XPress, and RagTime
- MS PowerPoint, Persuasion, DeltaGraph, and More II

E.g. on the IBM PC by:

- PageMaker and Ventura Publisher
- MS Word and Word Perfect
- Illustrator PC, Micrografx Designer, GEM Artline, Corel Draw, and Diagraph Windows
- Xerox Presents and Mirage

Again, anyone who wishes can write Color PostScript language programs for him or herself!

The colored circles

When you have made a closed path, you are able to fill the area with a color (area filling). This is achieved by the combination of the *setcmykcolor* and *fill* operators. You construct overlapping circles by applying different colors to the seven areas, see Figure 20.

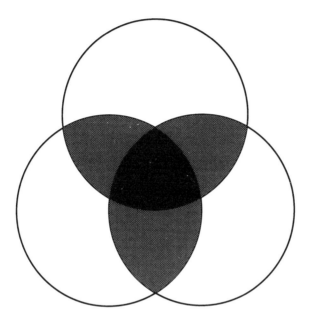

Figure 20 Circles with overlapping areas

The four setcmykcolor operands have to lie in the range from 0 to 1. The first operand specifies the cyan component, the second the magenta component, the third the yellow component, and the fourth the black component. Red may be generated by

```
0 1 1 0 setcmykcolor
```

The requirement for using *setcmykcolor* is simply access to a PostScript device which is able to print the colors. However, a black-and-white printer will generate equivalent gray shades. See Plate 1. *1 0 1 0 setcmykcolor* generates green.

```
%!PS-Adobe
%%BoundingBox: 100 100 316 316
%%Title: cmyk.ps
%%EndComments

% cyan-magenta-yellow-black color model

%%EndProlog

100 100 translate

        newpath
        108 144 72 0 360 arc         % cyan
        1 0 0 0 setcmykcolor
        fill

        144 72 72 0 360 arc          % magenta
        0 1 0 0 setcmykcolor
        fill

        72 72 72 0 360 arc           % yellow
        0 0 1 0 setcmykcolor
        fill

        % two-color areas:
        newpath                      % yellow+magenta
        72 72 72 300 60 arc
        144 72 72 120 240 arc
        0 1 1 0 setcmykcolor
        fill

        newpath                      % yellow+cyan
        72 72 72 0 120 arc
        108 144 72 180 300 arc
        1 0 1 0 setcmykcolor
        fill

        newpath                      % magenta+cyan
        144 72 72 60 180 arc
        108 144 72 240 360 arc
        1 1 0 0 setcmykcolor
        fill
```

```
                    % the black area:
                    newpath          % yellow+magenta+cyan=black
                    72 72 72 0 60 arc
                    144 72 72 120 180 arc
                    108 144 72 240 300 arc
                    0 0 0 1 setcmykcolor
                    fill


               showpage


          %%Trailer
```

The PostScript language not only supports the subtractive CMYK color model, but also the additive RGB model. The corresponding operator is called *setrgbcolor*. The three letters stand for: R = red, G = green, B = blue. RGB examples:

```
          0 0 0 setrgbcolor      % gives black
          1 0 0 setrgbcolor      % gives red
          1 1 0 setrgbcolor      % gives yellow
```

Characters in various reds

The character of any word may be rotated *(rotate)*, resized, made bigger, smaller, thicker, thiner, colored *(setrgbcolor/setcmykcolor)*, brighter, gray *(setgray)*, and so on. Also, the character may be combined with other characters or graphics and/or underlayed/overlayed by images.

In the example here, you first define the *rotationloop* routine to be called up five times by the *repeat* operator:

```
          5 { rotationloop } repeat
```

You save the graphics state *(gsave)* at the beginning of each pass and you restore the original graphics state *(grestore)* at the end of each pass. To the graphics state – an important PostScript idea – the following PostScript objects belong:

- The so-called Current Transformation Matrix (origin, scaling, and rotation of the coordinate system)
- The current clipping region
- The current color and the current gray level
- The current position and the current path
- The current typefont
- The current flatness
- The current line width, etc.

If you omit the *gsave grestore* operators in *rotationloop,* you would be forced to reset the current position at each pass.

With regard to the colors, at each pass the following PostScript operator is called up:

```
level 0 0 setrgbcolor    % red green blue components
```

While zeroing the green and blue components, we use the red components 0.8, 0.65, 0.5, 0.35, and 0.2.

Also, by using the *level* variable, we specify the gray level:

```
level setgray
```

This has the following impact: the more red, the less gray – and vice versa; *1 setgray* doesn't mean black, but white. See Plate 2.

The *%%BoundingBox, %%DocumentFonts,* and *%%EndProlog* structuring comments are provided too. The *%%EndProlog* comment shows where the script begins:

```
%!PS-Adobe-1.0
%%BoundingBox: 72 190 612 684
%%DocumentFonts: Times-BoldItalic
%%Creator: Richard and Peter
%%CreationDate: 5 Sept. 1989
%%For: EPS Book
%%EndComments

/inch {72 mul} def
/rotangle 90 def
/rotoffset 22.5 def
/level .8 def            % red component

/logosetup
   {(Times-BoldItalic) findfont
   [110 0 0 110 0 0] makefont setfont
   } def

/point  {0 0 moveto} def     % starting position
```

```
/rotationloop
   {gsave
   rotangle rotate
   level setgray          % gray level
   level 0 0 setrgbcolor   % red green blue colors

   (PostScript) show

   /rotangle rotangle     % make the rotation angle
   rotoffset sub def      % a little bit smaller

   /level level           % reducing the red color
   .15 sub def            % a little bit
   grestore} def

/logorot
   {gsave
        2 inch 3 inch translate   % user origin
        logosetup
        point
        5 {rotationloop} repeat
     grestore} def
%%EndProlog

logorot
showpage
%%Trailer
```

The following equations demonstrate the relationship between the RGB and CMYK color specifications. Since cyan is the absence of red light,

```
cyan = 1.0 - red
```

Similarly,

```
magenta = 1.0 - green
```

and

```
yellow = 1.0 - blue
```

PostScript extensions

The earlier versions of the PostScript language support color using the *setrgbcolor* and *sethsbcolor* operators, which enable the PostScript interpreter to paint filled regions, strokes, image masks, and characters in color. On black-and-white machines, these operators generate an equivalent gray shade, which is printed or displayed.

To support color more fully, the PostScript language was extended to provide the following functions:

- The CMYK color model: the *setcmykcolor* operator allows the user to set the current color in the graphics state to a cyan-magenta-yellow-black color directly. *Steve Roth* recommends this color input, because the color correction can be bypassed.

- Multiple color images: the *colorimage* operator renders a multiple color image. Its functions are analogous to the *image* operator, every 8 bits are represented as hex. XX. *colorimage* uses red-green-blue (RGB) or cyan-magenta-yellow-black (CMYK) color input.

- Halftone screen definitions: the *setcolorscreen* operator specifies halftone screen definitions – frequency and angle – for red, green, blue, and gray, or cyan, magenta, yellow, and black. It is the logical expansion of *setscreen* and takes the same three operands for each printing ink.

- Color correction: the *setcolortransfer* operator sets the transfer function parameters for red, green, blue, and gray. It is an expansion of *settransfer* to four color components. Furthermore, the *setblackgeneration* and *setundercolorremoval* operators are new (black is added as a component).

The PostScript language supports one-color, three-color, and four-color output devices. The color devices can be of two types:

- Binary: one-bit-per-pixel for each color component – typically printers
- Gray-scale: multiple-bits-per-pixel for each color component

A binary device uses halftoning to produce intermediate shades of its color components. If a device has eight-bits-per-pixel for a component, it is called a 'full gray scale' device that does not use halftoning.

Three-color devices may be either red-green-blue (RGB) – typically for displays and film recorders – or cyan-magenta-yellow (CMY) – typically printers. Four-color devices are cyan-magenta-yellow-black (CMYK) for color printers and color separation making devices.

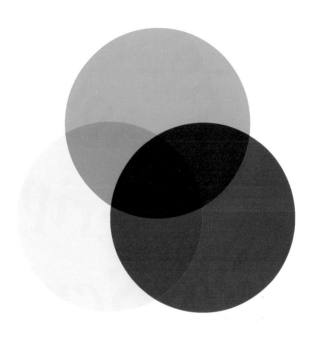

PostScript PostScript PostScript PostScript PostScript PostScript

Color separations

The output of the thermal transfer printers and of the other color printers may be used as color proofs, but unfortunately not as camera-ready copy. In order to produce long run color print products, color separations for cyan, magenta, yellow and black must be made, prior to the platemaking process. A highly accurate typesetter with a resolution of 1000 pixel/cm is required. The PostScript language may assist the production of color separations.

It is stressed here that the *setcmykcolor* operator may be redefined four times in a simple manner:

```
% cyan separation:
/setcmykcolor
 { pop pop pop 1 exch sub setgray }
 def

% magenta separation:
/setcmykcolor
 { pop pop exch pop 1 exch sub setgray }
 def

% yellow separation:
/setcmykcolor
 { pop 3 1 roll pop pop 1 exch sub setgray }
 def

% black separation:
/setcmykcolor
 { 4 1 roll pop pop pop 1 exch sub setgray }
 def
```

For each color separation, we use the *setgray* operator setting the current gray scale. The value of the operand has to lie between 0 (black) and 1 (white). The three other color components are discarded or 'destroyed' by the *pop* operator.

In the real world, the processing is much more complicated. For each process color, the screen dots have to be arranged at a different angle and in such a way as to prevent the appearance of disturbing moiré patterns. The choice of the right screening angle is dependent on the print production techniques being employed, the material and the experience of the operator.

Many graphics and publishing programs offer a color separation, for instance Page-Maker with PrePrint, FreeHand, LaserPaint Color II, Quark XPress, PixelPaint Professional, PhotoMac, ColorStudio, SpectrePrint; GEM Artline, Micrografx Designer, Corel Draw, Xenografics Mirage, PrePress, and Hell's ScriptMaster.

Open Prepress Interface (OPI)

The Open Prepress Interface (OPI) is an extension to the PostScript printer controller from Aldus. It was shown that essential data are lost when translating designed pages into the PostScript language. Pages coded in PostScript may be modified or corrected in a limited way only. Important information such as position, clipping area, scaling factor, or rotating angle of color images are no longer available in the PostScript language file.

As with each programming language, PostScript offers the option to generate comments. Comments are special information marked e.g. by the '%' sign in PostScript. However, the comments are ignored by the PostScript interpreter. They are quite useful in OPI. Aldus defined special OPI commands for all the image information required, but the PostScript interpreter treats these as comments only. For instance, the *%ALDImageFileName:* command addresses an image in the form of a separate TIFF file.

The Adobe Separator

Adobe offers the Illustrator bundled with the *Adobe Separator*. The Separator produces color separations for cyan, magenta, yellow, and black. If you are using the Pantone matching system the program produces a separate film for each Pantone color or converts the Pantone colors into the cyan, magenta, yellow, and black components.

In addition to the Illustrator PostScript file, the user may open a so called *PostScript Printer Description* file, that lists the specific features of the output device, for instance the standard screen frequency. A PPD file extract for a Compugraphic typesetter follows:

```
*% Adobe Systems PostScript(R) Printer Description
*% For "9400PS" version 49.3
*% Produced by "BuildPPD.ps" version 3.0 edit 57

*% Halftone Information ================
*ScreenFreq: "100.0"
*ScreenAngle: "45.0"
*DefaultScreenProc: Dot

*% Color Separation Information =====================

*%*DefaultColorSep: ProcessBlack.128lpi.1270dpi/
    128 lpi / 1270 dpi

*InkName: ProcessCyan/Process Cyan
*InkName: ProcessMagenta/Process Magenta
*InkName: ProcessYellow/Process Yellow
*InkName: ProcessBlack/Process Black
*InkName: CustomColor/Custom Color
```

Screening angles and frequencies:

```
*% For 121 lpi / 1200 dpi (7,7,4,11,11,4,11,0) ===

*ColorSepScreenAngle ProcessBlack.121lpi.1200dpi/
 121 lpi / 1200 dpi: "45.0"
*ColorSepScreenAngle CustomColor.121lpi.1200dpi/
 121 lpi / 1200 dpi: "45.0"
*ColorSepScreenAngle ProcessCyan.121lpi.1200dpi/
 121 lpi / 1200 dpi: "70.0169"
*ColorSepScreenAngle ProcessMagenta.121lpi.1200dpi/
 121 lpi / 1200 dpi: "19.9831"
*ColorSepScreenAngle ProcessYellow.121lpi.1200dpi/
 121 lpi / 1200 dpi: "0.0"

*ColorSepScreenFreq ProcessBlack.121lpi.1200dpi/
 121 lpi / 1200 dpi: "121.218"
*ColorSepScreenFreq CustomColor.121lpi.1200dpi/
 121 lpi / 1200 dpi: "121.218"
*ColorSepScreenFreq ProcessCyan.121lpi.1200dpi/
 121 lpi / 1200 dpi: "102.523"
*ColorSepScreenFreq ProcessMagenta.121lpi.1200dpi/
 121 lpi / 1200 dpi: "102.523"
*ColorSepScreenFreq ProcessYellow.121lpi.1200dpi/
 121 lpi / 1200 dpi: "109.091"
```

Adobe Photoshop

Adobe Photoshop is a high quality image enhancement tool that addresses photographic images. It is designed specifically for artists and desktop publishers. The program has a unique color separation feature called *automatic-trap*. Using automatic-trap, users can print separations directly from Adobe Photoshop or save images as Encapsulated PostScript files. These images can then be placed in page layout programs such as Page-Maker and Quark XPress. Macintosh users can also add type and line-art effects to images by placing Photoshop EPS files into Adobe Illustrator documents.

Photoshop reads PICT2, TIFF, MacPaint, PixelPaint, and the preview part in EPS files. Other files it can handle are the TARGA format, GIF, PIXAR, and Amiga IFF/ILBM files.

Emulating color PostScript

With regard to the above mentioned thermal transfer printers, only the QMS ColorScript has implemented the original Adobe page description language, while the Phaser printer from Tektronix works with a Color PostScript clone.

The *Howtek Pixelmaster* ink jet printer prints with melted color inks onto normal paper sheets, which is much cheaper than operating a thermal transfer printer. The melted ink is applied to the paper by a rotating printing head. The resolution is 240 dpi, the PostScript clone is named Script-It. Unfortunately, this color device is unable to print overhead projection originals.

Tektronix and *International Product Trading (IPT)* have overcome this lack by announcing its PostScript-compatible color ink jet printers. The resolution is 216 dpi or 180 dpi respectively. The Tektronix ink jet printer produces a page in two minutes and may be connected either to a personal computer or a Macintosh. The ColorPrint/PS Inkjet by IPT is based on a Sharp JX 730 printer.

As mentioned earlier, the emulation program *Freedom of Press 2.0* is able to output any Color PostScript file onto low-priced color printers such as the HP-PaintJet or NEC P6, and onto many film recorders. Freedom of Press operates under DOS and on Macintosh.

RIP-It for the IBM PC and MacRIP

RIP-It is a software interpreter by *Management Graphics* for the IBM PC that can output PostScript files onto film recorders of Agfa Matrix and Management Graphics. RIP-It supports color and uses the full resolution of film recorders (up to 4000 lines). RIP-It is sold together with the 35 fonts and can process additional fonts, including Bitstream and PostScript Type 1 fonts.

A similar program for the Macintosh user is *MacRIP* which can even display the Color PostScript graphics.

4.

Mixing PostScript Files

When mixing PostScript language or EPS files, it is always necessary to merge two or more files at the file handling level. The result of merging is a file which additionally contains the included files, finally this file is downloaded to the printer.

On one operating system, programs for positioning and scaling the included graphics may be available, on another platform, they don't. In this case, the software is based on the WYSIWYG principle, in that case, the user is forced to specify abstract formatting commands (markup-language approach). The Encapsulated PostScript (EPS) file format is particularly useful if you wish to include or import illustrations from other sources. This mechanism guarantees a high quality output of the illustration, but enables you to see and scale an approximation on your screen. All the Macintosh and GEM, MS Windows, or the Presentation Manager support the import of EPS files. See Figure 21.

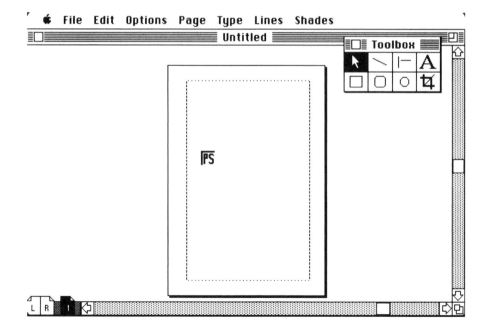

Figure 21   Embedding an illustration (PageMaker example)

With *Place* from the PageMaker file menu, an illustration or an image in the EPS File format may be embedded. Having specified the name of the EPS file, you click at the location where the illustration is to be positioned:

1.   Select EPS file
2.   Click the required location

Usually, the clipboard isn't concerned.

You can find Adobe's EPSF specification in Chapter 11.

The final solution is Display PostScript. Here, the same data stream goes to the screen *and* the printer. The correspondence of 'What You See' and 'What You Get' is 100%, except for the problem of matching RGB colors (additive, screen) with CMYK colors (subtractive, paper).

Bruce F. Webster writes in The NeXT Book:

'Once you've pasted in a graphic image (an EPS file), you can resize it, scaling it to be larger or smaller. To do this, double-click on the image, which will become faintly highlighted (a thin white band around the inside of the image). You can then move the cursor over the image, hold the mouse button down, and drag the cursor in or out. As you do, a thin gray box will appear, changing size as you move the cursor. ...'

The following letter (Figure 22) formatted by IBM or Waterloo Script contains a *segment include* markup command to embed a bitmapped logo:

```
.SI LOGO
```

The corresponding command in T$_E$X is:

```
\special{ps: plotfile logo.eps}
```

And in Troff:

```
\!include logo.eps
```

These commands concern the markup-language approach only.

Université de Zurich
Institut für Informatik
Winterthurerstrasse 190
CH-8057 Zürich

M. Jacques André
IRISA, Campus de Beaulieu
Avenue du Général Leclerc
F-35042 Rennes Cédex

Woodman'89

Zurich, le 4-1-1989

Cher Jacques André

Malheureusement je n'ai pas d'occasion de participer à votre conférence.
Mais si vous êtes d'accord, veuillez afficher mon papier.

Je vous souhaite mes meilleures salutations et beaucoup de succès avec
Woodman'89.

Dr. Peter Vollenweider

document "PostScript Applications and Encapsulated PostScript"

Figure 22 Letter with a bitmapped logo

Platforms

You will note, it is possible to combine PostScript files from various sources, i.e. to include images, graphics, and fonts into your documents. The keyword is 'Cut and Paste'. At the University of Zurich, the following combinations have been realized:

Publishing system   *Included PostScript files created on:*
UNIX with Troff   IBM MVS mainframe with plot programs;
                                      Apple MacDraw, Adobe Illustrator, CricketDraw;
                                      IBM's EPS-compatible scanner.

IBM VM/CMS with SCRIPT/GML
                                      UNIX/Troff eqn (mathematical equations) and pic (line graphics);
                                      IBM MVS mainframe with Versaplot, SAS/Graph, Tellagraf, Disspla;
                                      GEM Artline, MacDraw, MS Chart, Adobe Illustrator, Fontographer (our own fonts);
                                      EPS-compatible scanner from Agfa and IBM.

Macintosh RagTime/ReadySetGo
                                      IBM MVS mainframe with plot programs;
                                      MC View with Agfa Scanner;
                                      Illustrator'88, Fontographer, CricketDraw, and a dozen other Macintosh programs ...

The University of Zurich isn't a special case, other institutions have implemented similar solutions. The possibilities are nearly unlimited.

Also it is possible to operate a publishing software on the IBM PC or the Personal System/2 (for instance PageMaker, Xerox Ventura Publisher, MS Word, Word Perfect) and to include PostScript files from other sources. The *Personal Publishing System* of IBM is based on MS Windows and the PageMaker program:

Publishing system   *Included PostScript files created on:*
IBM PS/2 with Aldus PageMaker
                                      IBM MVS mainframe with plot programs;
                                      IBM's EPS-compatible scanner;
                                      GEM Artline, Illustrator PC, Typefoundry, Designer, Corel Draw, Harvard Graphics, ...

PageMaker, ReadySetGo, and RagTime are layout programs of the WYSIWYG mode. This means the user should see at the screen the document more or less as it will be printed on the output device. These programs don't force the user to struggle with abstract formatting commands.

PostScript operators used to embed

When a PostScript language file or EPS file is being imported, the illustration is positioned and additionally may be scaled, rotated, or clipped. In order to include graphics, you will use the *save, translate, scale, rotate, clip* and *restore* operators. The code is as follows:

```
%!PostScript code of the main document
  ...

save                  % save state

    200 200 translate  % translate origin
      .7 .7 scale       % reduce size
    % PostScript code of the included graphics
      ...
    (illustration included) = flush

restore               % restore original state

% the main document continues ...
  ...
```

This code first saves the state of the main document in the Virtual Memory of the printer (VM), then the origin of the coordinate system is translated and the graphic is resized. After embedding the graphics the original state in the VM is restored. Therefore the original coordinate system is valid, and the scaling of the graphics has no unwanted impact on the main document.

In the event that the illustration has to be rotated through 90 degrees, you have to issue a *rotate* operator. An example for an illustration rotated through 90 degrees:

```
save
    570 0 translate   % origin to the right
                      % because of rotation
    90 rotate
    % PostScript code of the included graphics
      ...
    (illustration rotated) = flush
restore
```

This example is valid for a A4 page, we have rotated the illustration through 90 degrees, counter-clockwise.

The clip operator

The *clip* operator does clip the graphics – like a cookie cutter.

```
save
      100 100 translate      % translate origin
      newpath
      0 0 moveto        250 0 lineto
      250 150 lineto    0 150 lineto
      closepath
      clip                   % clip graphics
      % PostScript code of the included graphics
        ...
      (illustration clipped) = flush
  restore
```

In this example we apply the *clip* operator. The graphics part outside the (350,250) bounding box is cut off.

See Figure 23.

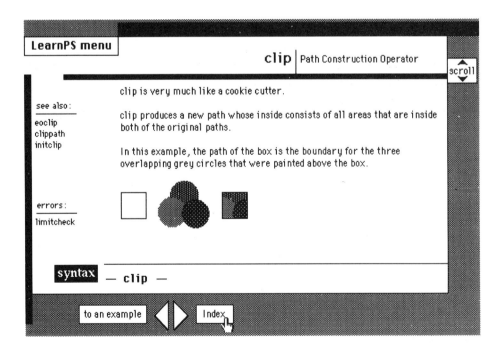

Figure 23 clip operator

PostScript as an interchange standard

In order to promote the PostScript language as an interchange standard, Adobe Systems offers two documents to the developer:

- **Document Structuring Conventions [4]:**

  Comment lines (beginning with '%%') – structuring the PostScript code, e.g. the %%EndProlog comment, and %%BeginProcSet and %%EndProcSet. A requirement of the structuring conventions is that one should be able to obtain the structural information from a page description without having to interpret or execute the PostScript program itself. A program is taken to be fully conforming to the current version of the file structuring conventions if the version identifier consists of '%!PS-Adobe-1.0' or '%!PS-Adobe-2.0'.

  The PostScript language code enclosed by the *%%BeginProcSet* and *%%End-ProcSet* comments typically represents some subset of the document prologue. The prologue may be broken down into many sub-packages, or *procedure sets,* which may define groups of routines appropriate for different imaging requirements. These individual 'ProcSets' are identified by name, version, and revision numbers for reference by a document management system. A document manager (spooler, server, or post-processor) may choose to extract these ProcSets from the print file in order to manage them separately for a whole family of documents. Note that an entire document prologue may be an instance of a ProcSet, in that it is a body of procedure definitions used by a document description file. The *name, version,* and *revision* fields should uniquely identify the ProcSet. The *name* may consist of a disk file name or it may use a PostScript language name under which the prologue is stored in the printer. In any case, these fields are used to identify the ProcSet to the document manager.

  Notice that this does not replace the *%%EndProlog* comment used in the original (version 1.0) document structuring conventions. It should still be used in the same manner, although now it is optional to provide the additional *%%BeginProcSet* and *%%EndProcSet* comments as well.

- **PostScript Printer Description (PPD) File Specification:**

  Gives information about device-dependent features of the printing system (paper sizes, available fonts, default screening, and so on).
  Example:

  ```
  %!PS-Adobe-2.0
  %%EndComments
  %%EndProlog
  %%BeginFeature: *PaperSize A3
  statusdict begin a3tray end
  %%EndFeature
  ```

The device-dependent operators are located between the *%%BeginFeature* and *%%EndFeature* comments.

In order to mix text, graphics, and images from various sources, the EPS File format serves as an interchange standard.

Some terms

In order to keep track, Glenn C. Reid defines some terms[3].

Document file   The document file (main document) is a PostScript program that may have another program embedded within it. It is typically simply the output of a page layout program or other document-producing software (publishing application).

Illustration   This is a program which executes *within* the context of another PostScript program. It need not truly be an illustration, but it is a good way to think of the relationship.

Print job   This refers to the PostScript file that is at the outermost level of execution. Note that this does *not* include the server loop. It is the first user-level print file.

Typically, the including main document is a multi-page document, while an illustration in the EPS File format doesn't consist of more than one page.

Michael Fryd gives four recommendations in his paper 'Writing Device-Independent PostScript', published in Roth[16]:

Context independence   Trust that the environment of the main document is correct. Rule: don't use init... operators, such as *initgraphics* and *initmatrix*. The initgraphics operator would reset the values in the current graphics state to their default values.

Device independence   Don't make any assumptions about the device your file will be printed on. Rule: don't use operators from the *statusdict* dictionary. The statusdict dictionary contains the device-specific parameters.

Page independence   Wrap each page with *save* and *restore* to make sure pages are independent. See 'PostScript Program Structure' in Chapter 2.

Spooler friendly   Follow *Adobe's Document Structuring Conventions* in the red book[2].

An embedding example

A paper created with Waterloo Script serves as an example of a document with embedded graphics, but it might just as well be a multiple-column document created by PageMaker, Ventura Publisher, or MS Word. See Figure 24 (Protext poster session).

The Waterloo Script Reference Manual documents the .SI Script command to include EPS files:

'SEGMENT INCLUDE names an external graphic segment of output to be included in the formatted document. The first operand specifies the name of a segment of external material to be included in the formatted text. This segment would normally be a graphic file, but it could be text as well. The Segment Include control word is only supported when used with the I3820 or POSTScript device option.'

In order to specify the bounding box and to place and scale the illustration, a number of operands is supported: *WIDTH, DEPTH, XOFF, YOFF, SCALE, ROTATE,* etc.

The document in the example was marked with markup tags and formatted by the Waterloo Script program. Additionally, the document contains a manually created PostScript program (logo), a line graphic generated on a mainframe (map of Switzerland), and a line graphic generated under Unix (pspaste). It is possible not only to mix text and graphical objects (vector graphics), but additionally bitmaps and images (pixel graphics).

Another example is the production of this book also formatted on the IBM mainframe by Waterloo Script. The document was marked with markup tags and segment include commands to embed EPS files and PostScript figures.

Some terms:

Export   generating EPS, save as..., cut

Import   including or embedding EPS, place, paste from...

ELECTRONIC CUT AND PASTE

PostScript is an excellent tool for merging text and graphics.

Script/GML and PostScript programming

This paper has been marked with Generalized Markup Language tags and formatted by Waterloo Script.
Let's incorporate a logo and the map of Switzerland:

PSpaste utility for merging text, graphics, bitmaps, ...

PSpaste is another troff preprocessor to assist in pasting images defined in the PostScript page description
language into troff documents. In order to combine pictures easily with the other troff preprocessors tbl,
pic or eqn, and to place pictures just like ordinary text, a picture is treated as a glyph with width and
height determined from the picture's bounding box.

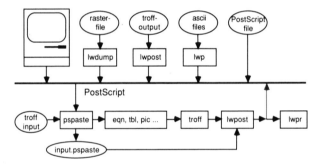

Using PostScript files generated by Macintosh and PC

1. The PostScript code or the Encapsulated PostScript File (EPSF) format can be generated by Fonto-
    grapher (Mac only), Publishers Typefoundry (PC only), Adobe Illustrator, FreeHand (Mac), Micro-
    graphx Designer (PC), GEM Artline (PC), and Corel Draw (PC).
2. Transfer the Mac/PC PostScript file onto the mainframe system (e.g. by TCP/IP Protocol)
3. Encapsulated PostScript (EPS) files are complete! The Apple macro library named LaserPrep is not
    required with Fontographer, Adobe Illustrator, FreeHand, Micrographx Designer, GEM Artline, and
    Corel Draw.
4. Modify the Mac/PC PostScript file as needed (positioning, scaling, rotating, cropping)
5. Output the PostScript file - with or without incorporating it in a document

Examples on Mac: Adobe Illustrator, Aldus FreeHand, CricketDraw, Agfa MC View, Fontographer
Examples on IBM PC: Adobe Illustrator, Micrographx Designer, GEM Artline, Corel Draw, Agfa PC
View, Publishers Typefoundry

- 3 -

Figure 24   Page 3 of a Protext poster session

Encapsulated PostScript Files (EPSF)

Nineteen eighty eight was the year of the PostScript page description language. The EPS
File format was stressed by the three companies Altsys, Aldus, and Adobe. Encapsulated
PostScript (EPS) can save vector graphics in a resolution independent mode (line art) and
also save gray scales (pixel graphics).

The EPS File format is quite useful for mixing PostScript files (text, graphics, image)
from various sources. It doesn't matter whether the user is located in a PC, Macintosh,
Unix, or mainframe environment, assuming there is some means of linking the machines.
Often he or she wants to embed an image or graphics generated on another system, see
Figure 25. The EPSF conventions are designed to allow cooperative sharing of files
between many systems using PostScript. Encapsulated PostScript (EPS) files are always
complete! There is no need of any further printer initializations, nor of downloading any
prep files or additional PostScript prologues.

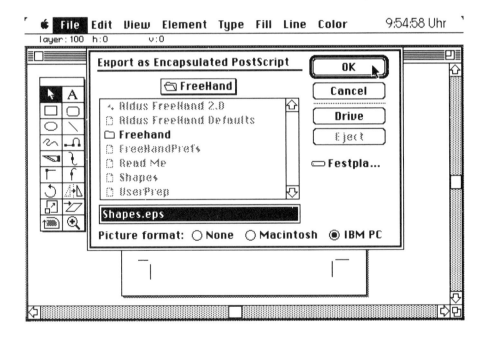

Figure 25 Generating EPSF (FreeHand example)

The EPS File format simply consists of PostScript command lines and a number
of additional comment lines for structuring the PostScript code. These comment lines are
introduced by the two '%%' characters.

Structuring comments:

```
%!PS-Adobe-2.0 EPSF-1.2
%%
%%    EPS header ...
%%
%%EndComments
%%BeginProcSet:

    procedures appropriate for a specific task ...

%%EndProcSet
%%EndProlog
%%BeginSetup
   setup ...
%%EndSetup
%%Note:

    document script ...

%%Trailer
```

Furthermore an EPS file follows:

Two rules

1. The file must be 'well-behaved'. Avoid initializations (init-operators) which can destroy the graphic state of the main document. Instead of using the init-operators use the *gsave – grestore* pair. Example:

```
gsave               % save graphics state
   0.5 setgray
   % gray scale
   fill
grestore            % restore
%
gsave               % save graphics state
   3 setlinewidth
   % line width
   stroke
grestore            % restore
```

```
    % again, you have a clean graphics state:
    fill
    stroke
       ...
```

Avoid the *initgraphics* and *erasepage* operators.

2. Declaration of the BoundingBox and the list of the used fonts. EPS header example:

```
    %!PS-Adobe-2.0 EPSF-2.0
    %%Creator:   ***** Roman *****
    %%Title: mathematical equation Ando-Modigliani
    %%CreationDate: 14:12:29 September 24, 1988
    %%BoundingBox: 0 0 590 300
    %%DocumentFonts: Courier Helvetica-BoldOblique
    %%+ Symbol
    %%EndComments
      ...
      ... (PostScript code) ...
      ...
```

The file must contain sufficient information about itself that an importing application can easily determine how to print it. In particular, the file must have the overall size of the illustration – by indicating the dimensions of a rectangle into which the illustration would fit. It must also have a list of all fonts used within the illustration, so that the importing program can make sure the fonts are available when it is time to print.

The showpage operator

The *showpage* operator is permitted in EPS files primarily because it will be present in so many PostScript files. It is reasonable for an EPS file to use the *showpage* operator if needed (although it is not necessary if the file is truly exported to another document). It is the including applications responsibility to disable showpage if necessary. The recommended method to accomplish this is as follows:

```
    save
        /showpage { } def    % dummying
        % PostScript code of included illustration
          ...
        showpage    % without any impact
    restore
```

This method will only disable the *showpage* operator during the execution of the EPS file, and will restore the previous semantics of *showpage* afterwards.

Operand stack and dictionaries

All the PostScript interpreter's stacks (e.g. the operand stack, the dictionary stack) should be left in the state that they were in before the imported PostScript code was executed. This is normally the case for well-written PostScript language programs, and this is still the best way to keep unanticipated side-effects to a minimum. If you have accidentally left something on one of the stacks, it is best to understand your program well enough to remove it, rather than issuing a wholesale cleanup instruction at the end, which will not only clear your operands from the stack, but may clear other objects as well.

It is recommended that the imported PostScript EPS file create its own dictionary instead of writing into whatever the current dictionary might be. The new dictionary is pushed onto the dictionary stack by using the *begin* operator. Make sure that this dictionary is removed from the dictionary stack when through (using the PostScript *end* operator) to avoid the possibility of an *invalidrestore* error.

If a special dictionary (like *statusdict*) is required in order for the imported PostScript language code to execute properly, then it should be included as part of the EPS file. However, it should be enclosed in very specific %%BeginFeature and %%EndFeature comments as specified in the Document Structuring Conventions. No dictionary should be assumed to be present in the printer.

Screen preview as approximation

Fundamentally, an Encapsulated PostScript file is merely a standard PostScript file with a bitmap screen dump optionally included in the format. Their purpose is to be included into other document makeup systems as illustrations, and the screen representation is intended to assist in page composition only. The bitmap is normally discarded when printing is done, and the PostScript segment (ASCII) of the file is used instead. Typically, any manipulation of the screen image that is performed by the user (such as scaling, translating, or rotation) should be tracked by the page layout application and an appropriate PostScript transformation should precede the encapsulated PostScript when sent to the printer.

The screen formats:

Macintosh   PICT format (QuickDraw)

IBM PC   Microsoft Windows metafile or TIFF (Tag Image File Format). The TIFF format exists in three 'flavors': CCITT compressed TIFF, packbits compressed TIFF, uncompressed TIFF.

In DOS, the EPS file itself has a binary header added to the beginning that provides a sort of 'table of contents' to the file. The header is followed by the PostScript program in ASCII text and the binary screen representation.

Importing and exporting EPS files

The best-known publishing programs capable of importing EPS files are Aldus PageMaker, Xerox Ventura Publisher, MS Word, Word Perfect, Quark XPress, and Ragtime from Germany. These support the WYSIWYG principle. The typical Macintosh user generates the EPS code by using the FreeHand or Illustrator '88 tools. Finally, the EPS file will be embedded by the PageMaker program: FreeHand → EPSF → PageMaker.

The IBM PC user will, on the other hand, generate the EPS language code by using Corel Draw: Corel Draw → EPSF → Ventura Publisher. A different IBM PC user may follow the route: Micrografx Designer → EPSF → MS Word.

In the PC world there is a number of conversion utilities to convert other graphic formats into EPS files: Hijaak of Inset, Hotshot Graphics by SymSoft, LaserPlot, SoftRIP, etc.

The modes of format conversion:

1. Pixel graphics → pixel graphics, for instance PCX → EPS.
2. Vector graphics → vector graphics, for instance PIC, CGM, HPGL, or GPI → EPS.
3. Vector graphics → pixel graphics
4. Pixel graphics → vector graphics (quite difficult).

1. The variety of the graphics formats makes the conversion facility very important. For instance you can use the *Hotshot* program to save a graphics window at the screen in the Hotshot format and then convert it into Encapsulated PostScript.

2. The ISO *Computer Graphics Metafile* (CGM) format under DOS and GPI under OS/2 are quite new. The Macintosh user may convert PICT files, for instance generated by MacDraw, into EPS files of the Adobe Illustrator (line art) by calling up the *Draw-Over* utility of Adobe. In the PC world too, some CAD formats such as PIC or HPGL may be converted into the EPS File format of Illustrator.

3. This mode is less interesting.

4. This mode is represented by the *Adobe Streamline* program which generates files in the EPS File format. Streamline is available on Mac and under MS Windows.

Desktop presentation

Concerning the Desktop Presentation software, so *Cricket Presents, MS PowerPoint, More II, Standout, Persuasion* (on Macintosh); and *Studio Work, AZartist, AZchart, DAPS* and other PC programs are able to import EPS files. The PowerPoint program of Microsoft strongly profits by importing, while its own tools are rather limited. Persuasion 2.0 has extensive business charting tools. You can import an EPS file by selecting *Paste from* from the file menu (PowerPoint), by selecting *Receive from* from the file menu (More II), or by selecting *Import* from the file menu (Persuasion).

Concerning the Business Graphics software, the following PC programs are able to export EPS files:

- Harvard Graphics (the well-known program)
- HP Graphic Gallery
- Mirage
- Pixie
- Lotus Freelance Plus

The software components capable of generating quality illustration graphics in the EPS File format are discussed in Chapter 6, e.g. Adobe Illustrator, GEM Artline, etc.

PC DOS programs supporting EPS files

Programs Exporting Encapsulated PostScript Files

20/20, 35mm Express, Agfa PC View, Arts & Letters, AutoScript, AZchart, Charting Gallery, Chem Base, Chem Text, Click Art Scrapbook Plus, Corel Draw, Cyber Chrome, DAPS, Design CAD, Diagraph Windows, Don Lancaster's Utilities, EasyFlow, Easylabel, Excelerator, GEM Artline, GEM Draw Plus, Generic 3-D, Graph-in-the-Box, Graphics Transformer Intergraphics, Halftoner, Harvard Graphics, Hot Type Laser Fonts, Hotshot Graphics, HP Graphic Gallery, IDRAW, Illustrator PC, Inset, Impressionist, ImageStation, Kinetic, LT200 MC, LT200 PC, Lumena, Mass-11 Draw, Mass-11 Database Manager, Mass-11 Graphic Processor, Math Type, Mathematica, MathGraph, Micrografx Designer, Micrografx Graph Plus, MicroStation, Mirage, PC-Slide, PC4096 Graphic System, Personal Composer, PictureThis, PinStripe Presenter, Pixie, Presenter PC, Professional Graphics Producer, PS Plot (HPGL translator), Publish It, Quantum Graphics, RIO, Samna, SAS, Score, SlideWrite Plus, Snapshot, SoftQuad Publishing Software, SpectrePrint, Studio Work, SuperImage, SuperVue, Ultimate, VCN Concorde, VersaCAD, VP-Graphics, Windows Graph Plus, Word-11, XED, XyWrite III Plus.

Programs Importing Encapsulated PostScript Files

Adept, Ami Professional, Archetype Designer, Autographix AutoVisual, AZartist, AZchart, Camera-Ready, Chemistry Library, Class Ad-db, Create! Form, CTextSetter II, DAPS, dbPublisher, Eroff, GML/PC, Hockney's Egg, Interleaf Publisher, Lotus Manuscript, MS Word 5.0, PageMaker, PC T$_E$X, PC-Write, Professional Writers Package, Scenic Writer, Spellbinder Desktop Publisher, Sprint, Studio Work, T^3, Textbase, TitusSetter III, Ventura Designer Stylesheets, Wave 4, WordMarc, Word Perfect 5.0, Xerox Ventura Publisher.

EPSF and halftoning

A reproduced image consists of an infinite number of gray scales, from white to 100% black. Because only black ink is used during printing, a method has been devised to simulate the gray shades: it is called screening. A screened image consists of a number of black dots. Gray scales are simulated by changing the size of the dots, while the number of dots per surface unit remains the same. The mathematical equation describing the relationship between screen density and number of gray scales is as follows:

$$screen\ density = \frac{printer\ resolution}{\sqrt{number\ of\ gray\ scales}}$$

The gray scales of an EPS image are not converted into halftone dots until they are printed. This is an advantage. An image with gray scales looks much better if the screen frequency of a high resolution typesetter is applied. It is even recommended that the *setscreen* operator is not used.

The usual laser printers have a screen angle of 45 degrees and a screen density of 60 lines per inch. The screen density of typesetters ranges from 90 to 120 lines per inch. Screening density in lines per inch and the resolution in dpi are not the same thing.

An image that saves its gray scale data offers two advantages to the professional designer:

1. Typesetter output will achieve high quality.
2. You can enlarge the image in your page make-up program without incurring the image distortion from which screened images suffer when enlarged.

But the disk space used to store images in the EPS File format is not modest.

To conclude: the EPS File format helps the image publisher to avoid a loss of data.

An EPS code describing images

Note, the following code obeys the EPSF conventions:

```
%!PS-Adobe-2.0 EPSF-1.2
%%BoundingBox:100 100 266.6 333.2
%%Creator:McView 1.0
%%Title:Peter
%%Creationdate: 11.02.1989  10:32 Uhr
%%TemplateBox:0 0 0 0
%%DocumentProcSets:Adobe_Illustrator_1.1 0 0
%%EndComments
    ...
    ... Prologue ...
    ...
doimage
2727272727272327232727272727272327272727
2B2727272727272727272B2F2F2727272B2B2B2B2B2B
2B272B2B2B272B2B2B2B27272B2727272B2B2B2B
2B2B2B2F2F2B2F2F2F2F2F2F2F2F2F2F2B2F2F2F
2B2B27272727272727272B272B2B232323232323
2B2B2F2F33333333373333373B3B3B33333737
    ...
    ...
%%Trailer
```

Generally an image is hexadecimal coded. Each 8 bits are represented as hex. XX. See Chapter 8 'Digitizing Images with the Agfa Scanner'.

In order to modify an image after scanning, the TIFF format may be preferred rather than the EPS File format. TIFF is the standard format supporting various ways of post-processing a grayscale scan (pixel manipulation). An image saved as an EPS file can be placed, scaled, rotated, slanted, and clipped only.

The file transfer

If you wish to combine PostScript files from different systems, you need to interchange data between various computers. The technical term is *file transfer*.

For the file transfer, not only a physical connection, a cabeling system, or a local area network is required, but also a standardized protocol for the transport of data. At the University of Zurich, the Kermit protocol of the Columbia University New York is used among others. The Kermit software is installed on almost every computer system: IBM VM/CMS, IBM MVS, UNIX, PC DOS, Apple Macintosh, ...

Although the file transfer by Kermit isn't fast, it is normally adequate, since PostScript files containing vector graphics are rather compact. The exception is formed by bitmapped images and images in the EPS File format.

However, there are alternatives to the Kermit protocol, e.g.:

- FTP on the base of TCP/IP and Ethernet.
- Unix to Unix CoPy UUCP.
- Protocols based on IBM SNA or DECnet.

A PostScript program consists of nothing but ASCII characters. Thus, the PostScript files also may be transported by Electronic Mail.

At the Zurich universities, the Zurich Academic Local Area Network forms the backbone for file transfer. The adapter T-boxes are of the *Localnet 2000* type and stem from the Hughes/Sytek company, California. Localnet alternatives: IBM Token Ring, Ethernet, Ungermann/Bass Net/One. Most terminals and PC's are attached to the local area network. The Macintosh PC's partly are interconnected by small AppleTalk/LocalTalk nets. A MultiTalk box forms a gateway between AppleTalk and Localnet 2000. MultiTalk boxes are sold by *P-Ingénierie,* Paris.

In addition, at the University of Zurich, CISCO routers and Applitek devices are installed in order to construct links and bridges between various Ethernets. The file transfer with FTP (based on Ethernet and TCP/IP) is much faster than with Kermit and therefore recommended for transferring images in the EPS File format.

PageMaker on Macintosh and IBM PC

The most widely used publishing program in the world is PageMaker by Aldus. The tools offered by PageMaker are the same on Macintosh and IBM PC, see Figure 26. The lower right tool is the cropping tool.

By using PageMaker you can create printed matter. At the display, various texts, graphics, logos, formulae, photographs, and images may be mixed in a simple way and printed on a laser or color printer onto paper or foil, or even on a laser recorder or typesetter. PageMaker imitates the traditional cut and paste.

Both on Macintosh and IBM PC (under MS Windows and OS/2), PageMaker is the best known desktop publishing program. With *Place* from the file menu, an illustration or an image in the EPS File format can be embedded. Having specified the name of the EPS file (by Select document), you click with the mouse at the location where the upper left corner of the illustration is to be placed, see Figure 21 at the beginning of Chapter 4. This is a quite natural way of embedding or importing. Having imported an EPS file, the illustration may be scaled down, enlarged, or clipped. See Figure 27.

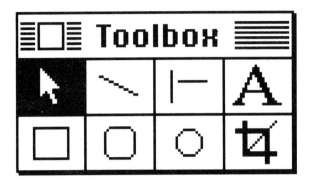

Figure 26 PageMaker toolbox

Resizing and cropping

The graphic may be resized in PageMaker by dragging at one of its handles. You may reduce/enlarge the width or the height of the illustration by dragging at the handle squares of the displayed bounding box (distorting). The bounding box indicates the illustration frame. See Figure 28.

You can trim or crop a positioned graphic with the cropping tool, from the toolbox. Cropping reduces the overall size of the graphic, but the part that remains does not change size. See Figure 29.

Figure 27   A PageMaker page with circle text imported three-fold

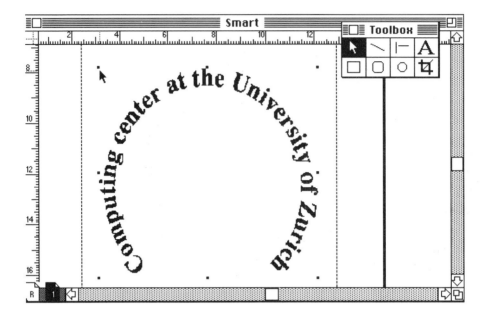

Figure 28 Bounding box with handles

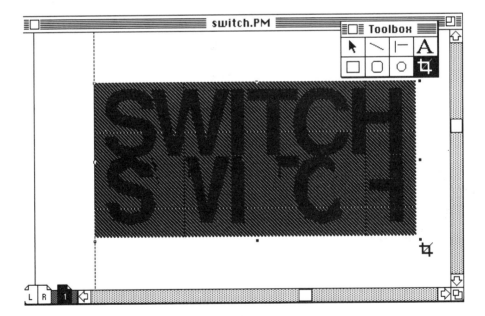

Figure 29 Cropping an illustration

Xerox Ventura Publisher

By using *Ventura Publisher,* the PC user interested in producing printed material such as magazines, manuals, and user guides can do so in a quick and low-cost way. The program offers the DOS user the following pull down menu's:

* Desk
* *File* → in order to include an EPS file (or load a text file)
* Edit
* View
* Page
* Frame
* Paragraph
* Graphics
* Options

Ventura Publisher can import EPS files. EPS files are even displayed at the screen if they contain either a TIFF or a Windows Metafile representation of the graphics. If not, a big 'X' is placed inside of the frame. When being imported, the illustration may be scaled, clipped, or rotated.

The version 3.0 under OS/2 can also display the EPS graphics at the screen.

Creating a PostScript file is recommended so that the final publication may be produced on a typesetter. First, 'PostScript' is to be chosen as the output destination: select the *Set Printer Info* command in the Options menu, then select *PostScript* as output device and *File name* as port or interface respectively. When printing, a 'select file' box is displayed, with this help you name the print file. Finally, the file may be sent to a PostScript laser recorder, since all data needed for recording are contained in it.

RagTime and Quark XPress

An alternative to PageMaker on Macintosh is RagTime, that unusually does not originate from the USA but from Europe (Hamburg). This program supports the import of EPS files. Such EPS files may be embedded by the *loading image* menu. The three important steps:

1. Define a frame as picture frame
2. Click into frame
3. Load image (specify the name of EPS file)

Working with frames also is known to the XPress users.

Also *DesignStudio* and *Quark XPress* can import graphics as EPS files.

When using PageMaker or one of the other layout programs you maintain complete control over all page make-up operations and immediately view at the screen how the printed page will look (WYSIWYG, What You See Is What You Get).

Microsoft Word on IBM PC

Another alternative for an embedding application is the *Microsoft Word* program. Not only can the Macintosh user specify that a keyed-in text is of the *PostScript* type, the IBM PC user can also apply this method. The included PostScript code is treated as a hidden paragraph. This makes it possible for instance to:

- Underlay the following paragraph with a gray area.
- Underlay a page with a 'watermark'.
- Print crop marks on every page.
- Draw a box around the following paragraph, see Figure 30.

Finally, the PostScript code – embedded in a Word document – can be output onto a PostScript-capable output device.

Example for an included code, that underlays a whole page with a light blue:

```
newpath
0 0 moveto          0 1000 lineto
1000 1000 lineto  1000 0 lineto
closepath
0 0 .33 setrgbcolor    % 33% blue
fill
```

If you download the document onto a black-and-white device the colors are simply converted to gray scales.

And a PostScript language code for producing a 'watermark' in 240 points and 10% gray:

```
/Roman /Times-Roman findfont
   240 scalefont def
Roman setfont
100 500 moveto
   .9 setgray
(@) show
```

Word version 5 – and Word Perfect version 5 – even do import files in the Encapsulated PostScript format and can display a screen preview. Hence, the version 5 not only is a word processing program but also provides many functions of a page-layout program.

.Z.C:\PS\COREL.EPS;17 cm;18,298 cm;EPS

Prentice-Hall, Inc., sells
THE „C" PROGRAMMING LANGUAGE book
written by Brian W. Kernighan and Dennis
M. Ritchie.

Prentice-Hall, Inc., sells
THE „C" PROGRAMMING LANGUAGE book
written by Brian W. Kernighan and Dennis
M. Ritchie.

Le livre THE „C" PROGRAMMING
LANGUAGE de Brian W. Kernighan et
Dennis M. Ritchie est publié par Prentice-
Hall, Inc.

Der Verlag Prentice-Hall, Inc., vertreibt
auch das von Brian W. Kernighan und
Dennis M. Ritchie herausgegebene Buch
THE „C" PROGRAMMING LANGUAGE.

Figure 30 Paragraph box and background

Initializing a PostScript printer by MS Word

Text processing and publishing programs such as MS Word and PageMaker generate multi-page documents though not Encapsulated PostScript files. This signifies that the IBM PC has to send on in advance a prologue to the PostScript printer. This prologue for Word is called *POSTSCRP.INI, PSCRIPT.INI* or the like.

The PostScript code of the prologue looks as follows, the structure comments are provided by the Word version 5.0 and higher:

```
%!PS-Adobe-2.0 ExitServer
%%Title: Microsoft Word Driver Prolog
%%Creator: Microsoft
%%CreationDate: Fri Aug 18 1989
%%BeginDocument: Microsoft Word 5.0 0
%%msinifile: POSTSCRA
%%EndComments
%%BeginExitServer: 0
   . . .
%%EndExitServer
```

ExitServer:

```
userdict /msdict known {stop} if
```

This line tests whether the name *msdict* is already in the user dictionary, by explicitly pushing *userdict* onto the operand stack and testing whether the name is present. If so, the *if* operator will execute the *stop* operator and end the current processing and wait for the next job. The name *msdict* is the name of a private dictionary that holds all the definitions for the Word application. The intention is to test whether the application has already loaded the dictionary.

```
% serverdict begin 0 exitserver
```

According to whether you delete the percent sign at the beginning of the serverdict line above – it introduces a comment line – or you let it be, the printer is initialized permanently or for the duration of the print job only. When the 'server loop' is quitted by *exitserver,* then the definitions remain valid until the printer is turned off.

Word 4 and Word 5 have the additional *mslinedraw* dictionary for defining simple line graphics. In this dictionary, the semi-graphics characters of the IBM PC are defined (not reprinted here). With the help of these symbols, you can stroke lines, boxes, etc.

```
%%BeginFont: mslinedraw
/mslinedraw 25 dict def
   . . .
%%EndFont

/LineDraw mslinedraw definefont pop    % since Word 4
```

Finally, the *definefont* operator names the font with the semi-graphics characters by the *LineDraw* name.

Portrait and landscape:

```
/PSl {msdict begin /ptop 792 def /sw 0 def
   /ftsz 12 def /smode 0 def /STh -3.6 def /fs 0 def
   /offset 0 def
   fonttable 1 get fontset E
   90 rotate 0 -612 translate save statusdict begin
   /waittimeout 360 def end} def    % landscape

/PSp {msdict begin /ptop 792 def /sw 0 def
   /ftsz 12 def /smode 0 def /STh -3.6 def /fs 0 def
   /offset 0 def
   fonttable 1 get fontset E save statusdict begin
   /waittimeout 360 def end} def    % portrait
```

Here, the page sizes for the landscape format *(PSl)* and the portrait format *(PSp)* have been set.

```
%%BeginProcSet: msdict 1.0 0
/msdict 100 dict def

msdict begin
```

MS Word uses its own dictionary called *msdict*.

Word operators

Now, the Word prologue defines higher PostScript operators that will be called up by the MS Word page descriptions. The defined *S* operator for instance serves for printing words. The *P* operator makes a certain movement or motion. In order to support the international character set, the *ReEncodeSmall* routine is defined.

```
/SLL {pop} def
/BD {STh ssc} def
/BU {STh neg ssc} def
/BN {0 ssy neg rmoveto} def

/P {exch msu exch msu neg ptop add moveto} def

/S {currentpoint 3 -1 roll sw 0 32 4 -1 roll widthshow
   smode 1 and 0 ne {false 1.4 ul} if
   smode 2 and 0 ne {true 1.4 ul} if
   smode 4 and 0 ne {false STh ul} if
   smode 8 and 0 ne {ldot} if pop pop} def
```

```
/C {1 string dup 0 4 -1 roll put S} def

/J {msu ( ) stringwidth pop sub /sw exch def} def

/PE {showpage ptop exch restore save exch
    /ptop exch def} def      % marks the end of page
 ...

/F {/ftsz exch def (-) stringwidth pop 2 div neg
 /STh exch def
 /ftcd exch def
 0 2 fonttable length 1 sub
   {dup fonttable exch get ftcd eq
    {1 add fonttable exch get fontset exit}{pop}
    ifelse
   }for
 E} def                                  % font change

/fontset {dup 0 get findfont /Eft exch def
         dup 1 get findfont /Bft exch def
         dup 2 get findfont /Ift exch def
         3 get findfont /BIft exch def
         } def                    % font set

/msu {20 div} def
/ssc {dup /ssy exch def 0 exch rmoveto} def
/ssm {dup smode or /smode exch def} def

/Cf {/Eft /Courier  findfont def /Bft
    /Courier-Bold findfont def
    /Ift /Courier-Oblique findfont def
    /BIft /Courier-BoldOblique findfont def} def

/ul {gsave /y exch def /dbl exch def 2 copy
   .2 setlinewidth
   currentpoint dbl {4 copy} if
   y sub newpath moveto y sub lineto stroke
   dbl {2.4 sub newpath moveto 2.4 sub lineto stroke}
   if
   grestore} def                        % underline

/PSe {restore end currentfile closefile} def % the end
   ...
```

Now, the encoding routine called *ReEncodeSmall* follows:

```
/reencsmalldict 36 dict def
/ReEncodeSmall            % this is the encoding routine
  {reencsmalldict begin
   /newcodesandnames exch def
   /newfontname exch def
   /basefontname exch def

   /basefontdict basefontname findfont def  % old font
   /newfont basefontdict maxlength dict def
   basefontdict
     {exch dup /FID ne
       {dup /Encoding eq
         {exch dup length array copy
            newfont 3 1 roll put}     % copy
         {exch newfont 3 1 roll put} % elements
         ifelse}
       {pop pop}    % discard FID
       ifelse
     } forall    % for all elements of the dictionary

   newfont /FontName newfontname put
   newcodesandnames aload pop
   newcodesandnames length 2 idiv
   {newfont /Encoding get 3 1 roll put}
   repeat
   newfontname newfont definefont pop       % new font
   end
  } def
```

The *ReEncodeSmall* routine has been defined.

The 'encoding vector'

Here, an important part of the prologue follows, what is the so-called 'encoding vector'. The encoding vector is the mapping of codes to the graphical symbols. For the support of the German and French characters (for instance ä,ö,ü,é,è,à,ç etc.) the creators of the Word driver had to specify an own encoding vector. The vector named *foreignvec* and the now defined *ReEncodeSmall* routine will be used at the end of the prologue.

```
/foreignvec [
128 /Ccedilla
129 /udieresis        % german umlaut ue
130 /eacute           % french e aigu
131 /acircumflex
132 /adieresis        % german umlaut ae
133 /agrave           % french a grave
134 /aring
135 /ccedilla         % french c cedille
136 /ecircumflex
137 /edieresis
138 /egrave           % french e grave
139 /idieresis
140 /icircumflex
141 /igrave
142 /Adieresis
143 /Aring
144 /Eacute
145 /oe
146 /AE
147 /ocircumflex
148 /odieresis        % german umlaut oe
149 /ograve
150 /ucircumflex
151 /ugrave
152 /ydieresis
153 /Odieresis
154 /Udieresis

155 /cent
156 /sterling         % british
157 /yen
159 /florin
160 /aacute
161 /iacute
162 /oacute
163 /uacute
    ...
174 /guillemotleft
175 /guillemotright
225 /germandbls        % german double s
249 /bullet
] def
```

Now we invoke the *ReEncodeSmall* routine repeatedly and each time use the *foreignvec* encoding vector as its operand:

```
/Courier /Courier-Foreign foreignvec ReEncodeSmall
/Courier-Bold
/Courier-Bold-Foreign foreignvec ReEncodeSmall
/Courier-Oblique
/Courier-Oblique-Foreign foreignvec ReEncodeSmall
/Courier-BoldOblique
/Courier-BoldOblique-Foreign foreignvec ReEncodeSmall
/Helvetica /Helvetica-Foreign foreignvec ReEncodeSmall
/Helvetica-Bold
/Helvetica-Bold-Foreign foreignvec ReEncodeSmall
/Helvetica-Oblique
/Helvetica-Oblique-Foreign foreignvec ReEncodeSmall
/Helvetica-BoldOblique
/Helvetica-BoldOblique-Foreign foreignvec
                                   ReEncodeSmall
/AvantGarde-Book
/AvantGarde-Book-Foreign foreignvec ReEncodeSmall
/AvantGarde-Demi
/AvantGarde-Demi-Foreign foreignvec ReEncodeSmall
   . . .
/ZapfChancery-MediumItalic
/ZapfChancery-MediumItalic-Foreign
foreignvec ReEncodeSmall
```

The names of the newly created fonts with the international character sets all carry a name with the *-Foreign* or *-F* suffix. In the case of fonts licensed from Bitstream:

```
/Zapf-Humanist-Roman
/Zapf-Humanist-Roman-F foreignvec ReEncodeSmall
/Zapf-Humanist-Italic
/Zapf-Humanist-Italic-F foreignvec ReEncodeSmall
   . . .
```

On the personal computer, the small umlauts (ä, ö, ü) received the codes 132 (octal 204), 148 (octal 224), and 129 (octal 201); and the French symbols é, à, ç, è received the codes 130 (octal 202), 133 (octal 205), 135 (octal 207), and 138 (octal 212) respectively.

In the output text (page descriptions), MS Word encrypts the umlauts and the French symbols in the octal coded mode. Examples:

```
(Andr\202) S            % André
(Montr\202al) S         % Montréal
(Z\201rich) S           % Zürich
(Schw\204bisch) S       % Schwäbisch
```

In the following table, the available PostScript fonts are listed and numbered:

```
/fonttable
  [0 [/Courier-Foreign /Courier-Bold-Foreign
   /Courier-Oblique-Foreign
   /Courier-BoldOblique-Foreign]
   8 [/Helvetica-Foreign /Helvetica-Bold-Foreign
   /Helvetica-Oblique-Foreign
   /Helvetica-BoldOblique-Foreign]
   9 [/AvantGarde-Book-Foreign
   /AvantGarde-Demi-Foreign
   /AvantGarde-BookOblique-Foreign
   /AvantGarde-DemiOblique-Foreign]
   10 [/Helvetica-Narrow-Foreign
   /Helvetica-Narrow-Bold-Foreign
   /Helvetica-Narrow-Oblique-Foreign
   /Helvetica-Narrow-BoldOblique-Foreign]
   16 [/Bookman-Light-Foreign /Bookman-Demi-Foreign
   /Bookman-LightItalic-Foreign
   /Bookman-DemiItalic-Foreign]
   24 [/Times-Roman-Foreign /Times-Bold-Foreign
   /Times-Italic-Foreign /Times-BoldItalic-Foreign]
   25 [/NewCenturySchlbk-Roman-Foreign
   /NewCenturySchlbk-Bold-Foreign
   /NewCenturySchlbk-Italic-Foreign
   /NewCenturySchlbk-BoldItalic-Foreign]
   26 [/Palatino-Roman-Foreign /Palatino-Bold-Foreign
   /Palatino-Italic-Foreign
   /Palatino-BoldItalic-Foreign]
   50 [/ZapfChancery-MediumItalic-Foreign
   /ZapfChancery-MediumItalic-Foreign
   /ZapfChancery-MediumItalic-Foreign
   /ZapfChancery-MediumItalic-Foreign]
   56 [/Symbol /Symbol /Symbol /Symbol]
   57 [/LineDraw /LineDraw /LineDraw /LineDraw]
   60 [/ZapfDingbats /ZapfDingbats /ZapfDingbats
       /ZapfDingbats]
  ] def
```

The semi-graphics font with number 57 is only defined since version 4. If in addition you want to use a font licensed from Bitstream for instance and download it onto the printer, this font gets the number 1:

```
1 [/Zapf-Humanist-Roman-F /Zapf-Humanist-Bold-F
/Zapf-Humanist-Italic-F
/Zapf-Humanist-Bold-Italic-F]
% Bitstream Fontware
```

A script generated by MS Word

A typical script, generated by Word 4 on an IBM-compatible PC, follows:

```
PSp 15819 SFL
PE                                    % blank page

2552 2621 P 6917 SLL
2552 5801 P 6917 SLL 24 18 F
                        % font number 24, in 18 point
() S 720 J (  Where) S 90 J ( you are working) S
2552 6101 P 6917 SLL
2552 6401 P 6917 SLL
2552 6701 P 6917 SLL 24 18 F () S 720 J (   there) S
90 J ( is enough food,) S
2552 7001 P 6917 SLL
2552 7301 P 6917 SLL
2552 7601 P 6917 SLL 24 18 F () S 720 J (  where) S
90 J ( you deal with words) S
2552 7901 P 6917 SLL
2552 8201 P 6917 SLL
2552 8501 P 6917 SLL 24 18 F () S 720 J (   there) S
90 J ( is shortage) S
2552 10001 P 6917 SLL 1 8 F   % font 1 in 8 point
() S 720 J ( ) S
( ) S 1 10 F (P) S 1 8 F (ROVERBS) S () S
44 J ( ) S 1 10 F (S) S 1 8 F (OLOMON) S
( ) S 1 10 F (14:23) S
0 12884 P 9469 SLL 9108 J ( ) S 8 10 F (-) S
56 J ( ) S (5) S ( -) S
PE                                    % end of page
```

```
2552 2621 P 6917 SLL
0 12884 P 11907 SLL 2544 J ( ) S 8 10 F (-) S
56 J ( ) S (6) S ( -) S
PE                                    % end of page


2552 2621 P 6917 SLL 1 11 F
                                    % font 1 in 11 point
(Mein) S 72 J ( herzlicher) S 84 J ( Dank) S
72 J ( geb\201hrt) S 84 J ( allen,) S
72 J ( deren) S 84 J
( Fragen) S 72 J ( im) S 84 J ( rechten) S
72 J ( Augenblick) S
 ...
PE                                    % end of page
```

The Word operator *F* specifies in which font and in which point size a text will be set. The font number 1 signals that you want to use your own downloaded font.

```
2552 2621 P 6917 SLL
0 12884 P 11907 SLL 2544 J ( ) S
8 10 F (-) S 56 J ( ) S (8) S ( -) S
PE                                    % end of page


2552 2621 P 6917 SLL 1 10 F
                                    % font 1 in 10 point
() S 55 J ( 1.) S
1076 J ( ) S B (Eingangs\201berlegung) S
E () S 55 J ( ) S 0 LL 3504 J ( ) S LE () S
55 J ( 13) S
2552 3161 P 6917 SLL 1 10 F () S 55 J ( 2.) S
1076 J ( ) S B (Wissen) S 55 J ( und Algorith) S
E B (mus: ein erl\204uterndes
Beispiel) S E ( ) S 0 LL 804 J ( ) S
LE () S 55 J ( 17) S
2552 3461 P 6917 SLL 1 10 F () S
55 J ( 2.1) S 966 J ( ) S
288 J ( Theoretischer) S 55 J ( Exkurs ) S
0 LL 3252 J ( ) S LE () S 55 J
( 20) S
2552 3761 P 6917 SLL 1 10 F () S
55 J ( 2.2) S 966 J ( ) S 288 J ( Die) S
55 J ( Praxis-Perspektive ) S 0 LL 3120 J ( ) S
LE () S 55 J ( 22) S
2552 4061 P 6917 SLL 1 10 F () S
```

```
55 J ( 2.3) S 966 J ( ) S 288 J ( Revision) S
55 J ( des Beispie) S (ls ) S 0 LL 3180 J ( ) S
LE () S 55 J ( 24) S
2552 4361 P 6917 SLL 1 10 F () S
55 J ( 2.3.1) S 801 J ( ) S 288 J ( Zeichen) S
55 J ( vs. Buchstabe ) S 0 LL 2832 J ( ) S LE () S
55 J ( 24) S
2552 4661 P 6917 SLL 1 10 F () S 55 J ( 2.3.2) S
801 J ( ) S 288 J ( Token) S 55 J ( vs. Wort ) S
0 LL 3420 J ( ) S LE () S 55 J (
27) S
2552 4961 P 6917 SLL 1 10 F () S 55 J ( 2.3.3) S
801 J ( ) S 288 J ( Liste) S
55 J ( vs. Inventar ) S 0 LL 3312 J ( ) S LE () S
55 J ( 28) S
  ...
PE                              % end of page
```

The occurence of the *PE* Word operator shows where the page break occurs. But MS Word generates the PE operator only, when you choose 'page' from the printing menu. The end of the script is marked by:

```
PE PSe    % end of the document
```

A part of the result (proverb of Solomon)

For enlightenment, refer to the Proverbs. See Figure 31.

'Where you are working there is enough food, where you deal with words (advices) there is shortage.'

Word Perfect on the IBM PC

Word Perfect can also output onto page printers. As all PostScript drivers do, the Word Perfect driver first sends a prologue down to the PostScript device. Having initialized a page printer that way, it can process the same data stream as a wheel printer. Hence, the PostScript device emulates the daisy wheel printer.

Where you are working

there is enough food,

where you deal with words

there is shortage

PROVERBS SOLOMON 14:23

Figure 31   A proverb of Solomon

A script example generated by Word Perfect

```
         . . .
%%EndProlog
wpdict begin
```

Word Perfect uses its own dictionary called *wpdict*.

```
_bd letter _bp    % begin page
0 13200 10200 _ornt
/Times-RomanR 600 _ff
0 13200 10200 _ornt 1945 11820 _m
/Times-BoldR 765 _ff

-8 _rm (I)_S -7 _rm -8 _rm (M)_S -7 _rm -8 _rm (M)_S
-7 _rm -8 _rm (U)_S -7 _rm -8 _rm (N)_S -7 _rm
-8 _rm (O)_S -7 _rm -8 _rm (L)_S
-7 _rm -8 _rm (O)_S -7 _rm -8 _rm (G)_S -7 _rm
-8 _rm (I)_S -7 _rm -8 _rm (S)_S -7 _rm -8 _rm (C)_S
-7 _rm -8 _rm (H)_S -7 _rm -8 _rm (E)_S -7 _rm 99 _rm
-8 _rm (U)_S -7 _rm -8 _rm (N)_S -7 _rm
-8 _rm (D)_S -7 _rm 99 _rm -8 _rm
(M)_S -7 _rm -8 _rm (O)_S -7 _rm -8 _rm (L)_S
-7 _rm -8 _rm (E)_S -7 _rm -8 _rm (K)_S
-7 _rm -8 _rm (U)_S -7 _rm -8 _rm (L)_S
-7 _rm -8 _rm (A)_S -7 _rm -8 _rm (R)_S
-7 _rm -8 _rm (B)_S -7 _rm -8 _rm (I)_S -7 _rm -8
_rm (O)_S -7 _rm -8 _rm (L)_S -7 _rm -8 _rm (O)_S
-7 _rm -8 _rm (G)_S -7 _rm -8 _rm (I)_S -7 _rm -8 _rm
(S)_S -7 _rm -8 _rm (C)_S -7 _rm -8 _rm (H)_S -7 _rm
-8 _rm (E)_S -7 _rm
/Times-BoldR 600 _ff

78 _rm /Times-RomanR 600 _ff

2295 11403 _m
/Times-BoldR 765 _ff

-8 _rm (U)_S -7 _rm -8 _rm (N)_S -7 _rm -8 _rm (T)_S
   ...
```

The _m and _rm operators predefined in the prologue perform an absolute or a relative motion respectively.

```
4972 8973 _m
(zur)_S 3242 8646 _m
(Erlangung)_S 83 _rm (der)_S
83 _rm (Philosophischen)_S
83 _rm (Doktorw)_S (\027)_S (rde)_S 4553 8319 _m
(vorgelegt)_S 83 _rm (der)_S 3967 7992 _m
(Philosophischen)_S 83 _rm (Fakult)_S (\334)_S (t)_S
83 _rm (II)_S 4972 7665 _m
(der)_S 4348 7338 _m
(Universit)_S (\334)_S (t)_S 83 _rm (Z)_S
(\027)_S (rich)_S 4950 5703 _m
(von)_S 4217 5376 _m
/Times-BoldR 600 _ff

-6 _rm (C)_S -6 _rm -6 _rm (O)_S -6 _rm
-6 _rm (R)_S -6 _rm -6 _rm (N)_S -6 _rm
-6 _rm (E)_S -6 _rm -6 _rm (L)_S -6 _rm -6 _rm (I)_S
-6 _rm -6 _rm (A)_S -6 _rm 78 _rm -6 _rm (B)_S
-6 _rm -6 _rm (I)_S -6 _rm -6 _rm (N)_S -6 _rm
-6 _rm (D)_S -6 _rm -6 _rm (E)_S -6 _rm
-6 _rm (R)_S -6 _rm /Times-RomanR 600 _ff

4642 5049 _m
(von)_S 83 _rm (Z)_S (\027)_S (rich)_S 3060 3741 _m
(Begutachtet)_S 83 _rm (von)_S 83 _rm
(Herrn)_S 83 _rm (Prof.)_S 83 _rm (Dr.)_S
83 _rm (H.)_S 83 _rm (R.)_S 83 _rm (Bosshard)_S 4592
1779 _m
(Z)_S (\027)_S (rich)_S 83 _rm (1989)_S
3751 1452 _m


_ep              % end of page
```

The WP script isn't an EPS file since it doesn't describe a single illustration, but a multi-page document.

Word Perfect 5.0 lets you include graphics in the EPS File format in your documents.

GEM or Ventura as an embedding application

As earlier mentioned, GEM or Ventura Publisher also can exercise the function of the importing application on the IBM PC. GEM itself provides a rather compact PostScript prologue. The predefined PostScript routines allow the drawing of objects (circle, arrow, etc.) and support the usage of the extended character set with the German umlauts, the French symbols, the pound sterling symbol, etc.

The PostScript prologue provided by GEM

This GEM prologue consists of 250 command lines – the 1988 version of rather more – and hence is shortened. The same prologue is used by Xerox Ventura Publisher.

```
%!PS-Adobe-1.0
%%Title: GEM Document
%%Creator: GEM
%%Pages: (atend)
%%BoundingBox: 0 0 575 755
%%EndComments
% Copyright (C) Digital Research, Inc. 1987.
% All rights reserved.

systemdict /setpacking known
{/svp currentpacking def true setpacking} if
```

First-generation PostScript printers don't yet know the *setpacking* operator. By 'packing' of the procedures you can conserve space in the printer memory (VM).

```
/gemdict 250 dict def
gemdict begin      % this is the GEM dictionary
```

According to the conventions, GEM puts its PostScript definitions into an own dictionary.

```
/bd {bind def} bind def
/ed {exch def} bind def

% User defined Start of Page procedure:
% this operator will be executed
% at the beginning of each page output by GEM
% and is provided to allow
% user-defined page initialization.

/UserSoP {} bd
```

GEM enables the user to open each page by his or her own PostScript routine named *UserSoP*. That way, the pages may be supplemented for instance by a page header, a company logo, or a 'watermark'.

bd means *bind def.*

The 1988 prologue version of GEM or Ventura Publisher is supplemented by halftone screen spot function procedures:

```
% Halftone screen spot function procedure array:
% this array is indexed into as follows:
% 0 = dot screen, 1 = line screen, 2 = ellipse screen,
% 3 = custom (user-definable) screen.

/ScreenProc[

  { % Dot screen
    abs exch abs 2 copy add 1 gt{
    1 sub dup mul exch 1 sub dup mul add 1 sub}{
    dup mul exch dup mul add 1 exch sub}ifelse}bind

  { % Line screen
    pop}bind

  { % Ellipse screen
    dup 5 mul 8 div mul exch dup mul
    exch add sqrt 1 exch sub}bind

  { % Custom screen
    dup mul exch dup mul add sqrt 1 exch sub}bind
  ]def
```

These procedures may be invoked by the *setscreen* operator in order to modify the screening of images (only since 1988 prologue version). This operator sets the current halftone definition in the graphics state.

A PostScript prologue consists of nothing else but definitions and isn't reprinted here.

```
    . . .
    . . .
    . . .
end
systemdict /setpacking known {svp setpacking} if
%%EndProlog
```

In the prologue, a series of higher PostScript operators such as *path, circle,* or *doarrow* have been predefined. The *%%EndProlog* comment marks the end of the prologue section and the beginning of the script section of the document.

Finally, the GEM or Ventura script can address single objects (line, circle, arc) in a simple way and thereby realize the page descriptions.

The PostScript example generated by GEM

See Figure 32, the K+K company logo. The two 'K' letters signify only the initials of the two company founders.

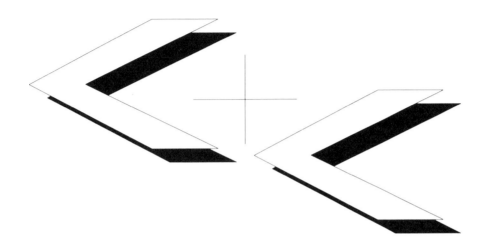

Figure 32 The K+K company logo

```
userdict /gemdict known not
    {/Times-Roman findfont 12 scalefont
    setfont newpath 72 700 moveto
    (Error:
    the GEM PostScript preamble is not available)show
    newpath 72 686 moveto
    (  on your printer.
    Pre-download the preamble or include it with)show
    newpath 72 672 moveto
    (your print job.)show
    newpath 72 658 moveto
```

```
     (This print job has been aborted.)show
  showpage stop} if   % checks whether dictionary exists
```

First it checks whether the PostScript interpreter knows the *gemdict* dictionary or not. If it does, everything is 'ok' and you can be sure that the printer has been initialized correctly. If not, an error message is issued and the print job is canceled. Before you make another attempt you must download the GEM prologue to the printer.

```
gemdict begin
648 828 0 1 GEM_INIDOC geminit
1 2399 2400 3150 false matinit
/fonts 35 array def /fpt 0 def
                              % enumerates all fonts
/GCourier addfont
/GCourier-Bold addfont
/GCourier-Oblique addfont
/GCourier-BoldOblique addfont
/GHelvetica addfont
/GHelvetica-Bold addfont
/GHelvetica-Oblique addfont
/GHelvetica-BoldOblique addfont
/GTimes-Roman addfont
/GTimes-Bold addfont
/GTimes-Italic addfont
/GTimes-BoldItalic addfont
/Symbol addfont

/GNewCenturySchlbk-Roman addfont
/GNewCenturySchlbk-Bold addfont
/GNewCenturySchlbk-Italic addfont
/GNewCenturySchlbk-BoldItalic addfont
/GPalatino-Roman addfont
/GPalatino-Bold addfont
/GPalatino-Italic addfont
/GPalatino-BoldItalic addfont

   ...
/GAvantGarde-Book addfont
/GAvantGarde-Demi addfont
/GAvantGarde-BookOblique addfont
/GAvantGarde-DemiOblique addfont
/GZapfChancery-MediumItalic addfont
/ZapfDingbats addfont
save mark
```

The names of the newly created fonts with the international character sets all carry the *G* prefix. The small umlauts ä, ö, and ü have the octal codes 204, 224, and 201. And the French symbols é, à, ç, and è, the octal codes 202, 205, 207, and 212 respectively.

GEM or Ventura Publisher also code these symbols octally. Examples:

```
(Andr\202) show          % André
(Montr\202al) show       % Montréal
(Schw\204bisch) show     % Schwäbisch
(Z\201rich) show         % Zürich
```

Now the script of the document describing the company logo follows:

```
%Begin page
UserSoP    % calling the Start of Page user exit
initclip 75 3074 2324 3074
2324 75 75 75 np mto lto lto lto clip np
                    % introduction
  2005 1312 1734 1887 1462 1312 1462 1600
1734 2133 2005 1600 6 2005 1312 path
gs 0 8 div setgray
gs eofill % filling a closed path
  gr gr 0 setgray
2005 1312 1734 1887 1462 1312 1462 1600
1734 2133 2005 1600 6 2005 1312 path
stroke     % stroking path
2062 1391 1790 1966 1519 1391 1519 1678
1790 2212 2062 1678 6 2062 1391 path
gs 1 setgray
gs eofill % filling a closed path

gr gr 0 setgray
2062 1391 1790 1966 1519 1391 1519 1678
1790 2212 2062 1678 6 2062 1391 path
stroke     % stroking path
1705 337 1434 912 1162 337 1162 625 1434
1159 1705 625 6 1705 337 path
gs 0 8 div setgray
gs eofill % filling a closed path
  gr gr 0 setgray
1705 337 1434 912 1162 337 1162 625 1434
1159 1705 625 6 1705 337 path
stroke     % stroking path
```

```
. . .
. . .

0 setgray
1725 1500 1 1725 1050 path
stroke
%End page
showpage cleartomark    % clear stack
restore gr    % restore graphics state
```

Finally, the *showpage* operator outputs the current page. *cleartomark* guarantees that the operand stack is left in a clean state.

```
end %    pop dictionary
%%Trailer
%%Pages: 1
%%EOF
```

The *%%EOF* (End-of-File) comment signals, that the spooler – hopefully – will terminate the print job by control-d. This is valid with a serially attached device only and doesn't concern the LocalTalk.

> Neither GEM nor Ventura Publisher generate files in the Encapsulated PostScript format, but both programs can import EPS files.

A page description generated by Ventura Publisher

Most text strings are printed by calling up the predefined *fjt* operator.

```
/svobj save def
%Begin page
UserSoP    % addressing Start of Page
greset
-300 3806 2781 3806 2781 -301 -300
-301 np mto lto lto lto clip np
greset
-75 3581 2555 3581 2555 -75 -75
-75 np mto lto lto lto clip np
```

```
/tface 9 def
9 encfont


    ...

sf
920 2488 523 2 (PC - Grundkurs)fjt    % printing
1113 2077 137 0 (zum)fjt              % text...
877 1665 609 1 (neuen Holzverkauf)fjt
/tface 8 def
8 encfont

/txscale 1200 3 mul 72 div def
/tyscale 1200 3 mul 72 div def
sf
1021 954 322 2 (im August 1989)fjt
932 721 500 4 (\275 1989, Oberforstamt / J)fjt

greset -300 3806 2781 3806 2781 -301 -300
-301 np mto lto lto lto clip np
%End page
showpage svobj restore gr
```

The strings to be printed are enclosed by parentheses. *tface* specifies the selected font. *encfont* invokes the ReEncodeSmall routine.

PostScript files from the Macintosh

You wish to generate PostScript or EPS code on the Macintosh and import it into any electronic publishing or desktop publishing application. The publishing or DTP system may be an IBM PC, a PS/2 computer, the IBM publishing system under VM/CMS, a UNIX workstation, or a Macintosh II for example.

(a) Generating the PostScript code

With many good applications, an EPS file can be generated under the 'Save As...' or 'Export' menu.

The following applies to some programs such as MacDraw, Draw II, or MS Chart only: When clicking on the ok button of the printing dialog, you must press the command key and the letter 'F' simultaneously. This causes the Macintosh not to send the PostScript file onto the LaserWriter, but to save it to disk. See Figure 33 (MacDraw is used to create line drawings).

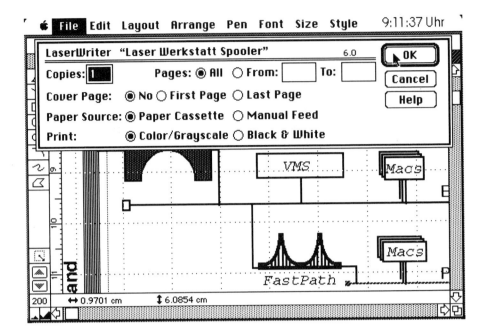

Figure 33   Draw II: pressing command key and 'F' simultaneously

Pressing command-F isn't necessary with Fontographer, SmartArt, TypeAlign, Illustrator, FreeHand, CricketDraw, and MC View, because you can instruct the program to generate the PostScript code directly.

(b) Transferring the PostScript code

The Mac PostScript file now is transferred onto the required target system, e.g. file transfer:

- Macintosh → personal computer
- Macintosh → IBM Personal System/2, or
- Macintosh → UNIX VAX

With regard to the basic character set, PostScript obeys the ASCII standard. But the German umlauts and other international symbols (French é, è, à, ç, etc.) are coded by four digits, for instance (Z\201rich) and (Andr\202). Please note, the encoding vectors differ on different platforms.

Self-evidently, the file transfer isn't needed if you want to embed the file in a publishing system on the Macintosh itself (e.g. PageMaker or RagTime).

(c) **With or without macro library**

In order to work properly, an EPS file never needs a supplement since it is generally complete.

The following applies to some programs such as MacDraw or MS Chart only: remember that on the target system (e.g. PS/2), the PostScript macro library, LaserPrep, from Apple is needed too, or possibly the AldusPrep macro library from Aldus. Each library contains some 800 lines of PostScript code. You can create a copy of the macro library – in addition to the PostScript file – if you press the command key and 'K' simultaneously (instead of 'F'). The macro library then has to be transferred onto the target system and downloaded as prologue onto the printer (before downloading the command-F file). Pressing command-K isn't necessary with Fontographer, SmartArt, TypeAlign, Adobe Illustrator, FreeHand, CricketDraw, and MC View, because these programs always use their own PostScript prologue.

It should be stressed here that the use of files created by command-F can raise some questions, since the LaserPrep file and the command-F file must match. And in real life, there are many different LaserPrep versions. The following typical message comes from a German user in Hanover:

'Hello Peter,

If you read the latest "INFO-MAC's", you will find out that my problem is shared by many people. At the Massachusetts Institute of Technology also there is a guy who nibbles at the same problem and doesn't know how to instruct the DEC LN03R printer, that it isn't longer basic PostScript but shortcut PostScript of Apple ... Something must be hidden in there, maybe in Apple's ROM. Well, I don't know, although I tested different Prep files – with and without the smoothing part ... The discussion shows that there is a general need for solutions to this problem. Obviously, it may only be a lack of information of some kind.

Yet there is a worldwide need to better understand which Prep files cooperate with which Laserwriter drivers and which printers, and/or why there are such difficulties. Thus, as you mentioned, PostScript is a universally interpreted language, and the technology should be standardized and should match.

So long ... Michael'

Some times, a trick can help: in the Apple LaserPrep file, the whole 'smoothing part' is deleted. The part to be deleted begins with the line:

```
currentfile ok userdict /stretch ... eexec ...
```

or in the LaserPrep 6.0 version with:

```
ok userdict /stretch known not and checkload
```

and continues until the end of the prologue. This part can be cut out and removed by using a text editor.

The best method to avoid these problems is using EPS files!

(d) Modifying the PostScript file

Modify the Mac PostScript file as desired (positioning, scaling, cropping, rotation). The standard PostScript operators are *translate, scale, clip* and *rotate*. See 'PostScript operators used to embed' on page 71 in this Chapter. In order to embed, the *showpage* operator has to be removed from the file to be imported because the *showpage* operator is called up by the publishing application in the main document. This is achieved best by dummying the *showpage* operator (as earlier shown).

If the PostScript interpreter issues a

> |_____Helvetica Font not found, using Courier.

or

> |_____Times Font not found, using Courier.

message, then you need to replace the '|_____Helvetica' and '|_____Times' font names with 'Helvetica', 'Times' etc. The basic PostScript font names don't have a '|_____' prefix. The prefix relates to Apple's encoding vector. By changing the names however, it may happen that the umlauts and other international characters (such as é, è, à, ç) are lost. This forces you to specify your own encoding routine and vector.

EPS effects by Emerald City Software

Adobe offers a PostScript editing program. It is called *SmartArt* and on the Mac, can be invoked as a desk accessory (DA) by any application. It allows you to rotate, slant, and distort text in any direction and to achieve various effects and colors, see Figure 34.

The result computed by the LaserWriter is displayed at the screen and may be copied via clipboard into the underlying application, e.g. into MS Word or Aldus PageMaker. If your program imports Encapsulated PostScript (EPS) files, you can save the effect as an EPS file and then import it into your document by using your application's *Place* or *Import...* command. In general, if you are going to print to a PostScript printer, Emerald City Software recommends using the EPS format whenever possible. All desktop publishing and many presentation applications can import EPS files.

The EPS file thus contains a screen preview computed by the PostScript printer and made available by SmartArt! You may also have stored a PostScript program as a standard ASCII text in a TEXT file type. If you have any PostScript programs as TEXT files, you can open them with SmartArt by clicking the *EPSF and TEXT* radio button at the bottom of the dialog box. In order to let SmartArt create a screen preview you have to specify correct BoundingBox information and erase the *showpage* operator from the PostScript program.

Figure 34 EPS effects by SmartArt

The bounding box

As any EPS file does, the EPS head generated by SmartArt always contains a Bounding-Box comment specifying the lower left and the upper right corner of the bounding box. For instance:

```
%!PS-Adobe-2.0 EPSF-1.2
%%Title: Centered Arc Text
%%Creator: Emerald City Software
%%CreationDate: 02/01/89
%%For:Smart Art
%%DocumentFonts: Times-Bold
%%BoundingBox: 130 172 470 470
%%EndComments
```

If you wish to reduce the bounding box, any importing application would clip the illustration. When the EPS file is being imported the *%%BoundingBox: 130 172 470 440* information would cause the result shown in Figure 35.

The upper edge of the box is not located at the 470 point position, but at the 440 point position. Note that the importing application always takes the *%%BoundingBox* in the EPS header as the 'truth', see Chapter 11.

Figure 35   BoundingBox reduced slightly

The clipping program

The importing application executes the following clipping program:

```
newpath

130 172 moveto
130 440 lineto
470 440 lineto
470 172 lineto
closepath           % bounding box

clip                % clip box
clippath stroke     % stroke box
```

This code is followed by the PostScript program generated by SmartArt.

TypeAlign

Emerald City Software – now Adobe Systems – offers another desk accessory producing text effects as EPS Files: *TypeAlign,* together with the Adobe Type Manager, can manipulate any PostScript font, including Type 1 fonts – a LaserWriter is not required. This DA lets you type text directly onto lines, arcs, and freeform curves. E.g. after drawing a freehand line, TypeAlign selects the text tool so you can type along it. The text can be kerned, colored, rotated, or distorted.

To copy your creation to the clipboard, select the pointer tool and select *Copy* from your application's Edit menu. So you can paste it into a document in your favorite application. In order to export to the Encapsulated PostScript (EPS) format, select *Save As* from the TypeAlign menu. TypeAlign displays a pop-up menu of the available formats: PICT, EPS and Illustrator. You can place Encapsulated PostScript files in any application which supports that format.

The following EPS code generated by TypeAlign sets the string 'Jupiter' along a freeform curve:

```
      . . .
    1.0000   1.0000   1.0000 0.0000 k
/_Times-Roman 48 0 0 0 z
[  0.9728 -0.2316   0.2316   0.9728 137.2177 125.9024 ]e
1 (J)t
T
    1.0000   1.0000   1.0000 0.0000 k
/_Times-Roman 48 0 0 0 z
[  1.0000   0.0000   0.0000   1.0000 155.4354 122.0000 ]e
1 (u)t
T
    1.0000   1.0000   1.0000 0.0000 k
/_Times-Roman 48 0 0 0 z
[  0.9877   0.1559 -0.1559   0.9877 179.3360 122.1284 ]e
1 (p)t
T
    1.0000   1.0000   1.0000 0.0000 k
/_Times-Roman 48 0 0 0 z
[  0.9438   0.3303 -0.3303   0.9438 203.0602 125.8857 ]e
1 (i)t
T
    1.0000   1.0000   1.0000 0.0000 k
/_Times-Roman 48 0 0 0 z
[  0.9438   0.3303 -0.3303   0.9438 215.3208 130.9508 ]e
1 (t)t
T
    1.0000   1.0000   1.0000 0.0000 k
/_Times-Roman 48 0 0 0 z
[  0.9950   0.0995 -0.0995   0.9950 227.8617 135.9400 ]e
1 (e)t
T
    1.0000   1.0000   1.0000 0.0000 k
/_Times-Roman 48 0 0 0 z
[  0.9908 -0.1351   0.1351   0.9908 249.1071 137.2750 ]e
1 (r)t
T

      . . .
U
showpage
%%Trailer
_E end
```

The prologue of an EPS file generated by TypeAlign contains the Adobe Illustrator procedure set. *z* invokes findfont, scalefont, and setfont. *T* marks the end of a text block.

Multi-Ad-Creator (Mac only)

The *Multi-Ad-Creator* program offers the Macintosh user another page make-up alternative. It is specially intended for composing advertisements and supports the four-color
separation of 8-bit color scans. EPS graphics can be imported and positioned. After this
you may translate, resize, crop, or rotate an EPS graphic, see Figure 36.

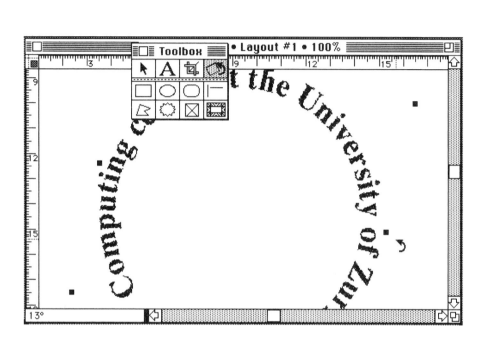

Figure 36 Rotating an EPS graphic

Ad-Creator files may be exported as EPS or PICT files. An ad can be saved as an EPS
file and reimported by Multi-Ad-Creator.

TeX and Encapsulated PostScript files

The *User's Guide to TeXTURES* by Blue Sky Research describes how EPS files may be imported by T$_E$X documents. The *illustration* command has to specify the name of the EPS file. The lower left corner of the illustration will be placed at the current T$_E$X position.

If the EPS file also contains a screen representation of the illustration, *TeXTURES* displays an approximation at the screen.

The alternative to *TeXTURES* is OzTeX on the Apple Mac or T$_E$X on the IBM PC.

Let's follow a discussion on the fonts topic between two net subscribers! Tony Scandora <B35048%ANLCMT.BITNET@Forsythe.Stanford.EDU> asked about outputting TeX to a Linotronic typesetter.

'1. Our group of TeX/LaTeX users has been using 300 dpi laser printers for a long time. Now we want to see important material printed on our 1200 dpi Linotype typesetter that speaks only PostScript, as far as we know. I can think of four ways to do it: compute the PK fonts for that magnification and use DVIALW. I suspect that computing the fonts may take a while and that PostScript files that contain 1200 dpi fonts may be pretty hefty. Has anyone done it? How bad is it?

Yes, I've generated the fonts at 1270dpi. For all 74 canonical CM fonts at all seven canonical \magstep's, a total of about 24 hours CPU time on a VAX 8700/8800 cluster were involved. The files are available from the Aston archive in the UK. I would acknowledge the kind donation of machine resources by British Petroleum Exploration to enable the generation of these fonts over one weekend.

2. Convert the METAFONT descriptions of the TeX/LaTeX fonts to scalable PostScript fonts and download them. Is that possible? Has anyone done it?

It's being done. I have no references to hand, but maybe ArborText (Michigan) and/or NorthLake are involved.

3. Come up with the font metrics for the standard PostScript fonts and use them. This would probably require a PostScript plain.tex and lplain.tex that would make DVI files that can only be printed on PostScript printers and would not look like documents that use the TeX fonts. I've heard rumors that this has been done. Would anyone care to substantiate same?

No problem. It's definitely been done. I will make PS-Plain available on the Aston TeX-Server if required.

4. Convince Adobe to add the TeX/LaTeX fonts to the standard PostScript fonts. I won't hold my breath for that one.

Nor I.'

5.

The Construction of the SWITCH Logo

This example has several levels. We will develop a logo, while proceeding from version 0 to version 1, to version 2, and so on. This example may stimulate you to modify, to extend, and to combine PostScript programs. SWITCH is the label for the Swiss Academic and Research Network (Teleinformatikdienste für Lehre und Forschung).

SWITCH logo version 0

How may the patterned characters, as shown in Figure 37, be described by a PostScript program? In order to do so, we use the *clip* operator. First of all, we construct the pattern for the background, i.e. the oblique strokes. The *Background* routine consists of a *repeat* loop, that calls up the *strich* (= line) and *sprung* (= move) routines and produces the stroked pattern. Now the *clip* operator cuts out a piece. This operator is well suited for filling characters or other forms with a pattern or names. After using *clip,* it is important to apply the *newpath* operator. Without *newpath* both the pattern and the outlines would be shown; and the outlines are not required. Finally, the defined *Background* procedure is called up.

Figure 37 The 'SWITCH' letters filled with a pattern

```
%!PS SWITCH logo, version 0
%%Title: switch0.ps
%%DocumentFonts: Helvetica-Bold
%%BoundingBox:
%%EndComments

/Bold /Helvetica-Bold findfont 100 scalefont def

/strich { 500 -500 rlineto } def          % line
/sprung { -500 496 rmoveto } def          % move
/Background { gsave
              150 { strich sprung } repeat
              stroke grestore } def

%%EndProlog

50 350 translate

gsave
    newpath
    0 0 moveto
    8 setflat
    Bold setfont (SWITCH) true charpath clip
                                          %  cut out

    newpath
    0 550 moveto
    1 setlinewidth
    Background
grestore

showpage
%%Trailer
```

The *%%EndProlog* comment marks the end of the definition section and the beginning of the script section of the document.

SWITCH logo version 1

In the next version of our PostScript program we are building an additional background and using the *show* operator to print the 'SWITCH' letters in black. In the *Background2* routine the strokes are slightly more oblique than in *Background*. The *Background2* routine consists of a *repeat* loop, that calls up the *strich2* and *sprung2* routines and produces the other stroked pattern. The usage of the *show* operator is based on the same font and point size as our *charpath*, the *Bold* variable means: Helvetica bold typefont in 100 point.

```
%!PS SWITCH logo, version 1
%%Title: switch1.ps
%%DocumentFonts: Helvetica-Bold
%%BoundingBox:
%%EndComments

/Bold /Helvetica-Bold findfont 100 scalefont def

/strich { 500 -500 rlineto } def          % line
/sprung { -500 496 rmoveto } def          % move
/Background { gsave
             150 { strich sprung } repeat
             stroke grestore } def

/strich2 { 500 -480 rlineto } def
/sprung2 { -500 475.9 rmoveto } def
/Background2 { gsave
             150 { strich2 sprung2 } repeat
             stroke grestore } def

%%EndProlog

50 350 translate

gsave
   newpath
   0 0 moveto
   8 setflat

   Bold setfont (SWITCH) true charpath clip
                                    %  cut out
```

```
    newpath
    0 550 moveto
    1 setlinewidth
    Background2
grestore

0 74 moveto
Bold setfont (SWITCH) show    % printing usually

newpath
0 550 moveto
0.1 setlinewidth
Background

showpage
%%Trailer
```

See Figure 38.

SWITCH logo version 2

In order to cut out the whole logo, in the next program version we are using an additional *clip* operator at the beginning of the script section (after the prologue). Having built a path *(newpath moveto lineto ... closepath)* we are able to write *clip* instead of *stroke*.

Furthermore, in the version 2 the line widths are modified:

```
    .4 setlinewidth
```

The operand means .4 typographical points.

The *setflat* operator controls the accuracy with which curved path segments are to be rendered on the raster output device by the *clip* operator. The choice of flatness value is a tradeoff between accuracy and execution efficiency.

Very small values (for instance 1 or less) produce very accurate curves at high printer time costs. Larger values (for instance 50) produce cruder approximations with substantially less computation. The values represent the maximum distance of any point of the approximation from the corresponding point on the true curve, measured in output device pixels, not in points! The 'setflat' parameter – as other parameters do – also belongs to the graphics state.

Figure 38   SWITCH logo, version 1

EPS comment lines

Note the structure comments:

```
%%Title: switch2.ps
%%BoundingBox: 100 350 500 500
%%DocumentFonts: Helvetica-Bold
%%Creator: Peter
%%CreationDate: 5 Sept 1989
%%EndComments
```

The bounding box encloses all the elements painted as a result of executing this program. All four values must be integers and represent the coordinates of the lower left and upper right corners of the bounding box in the default user coordinate system. While the *%%BoundingBox* comment is required by the EPSF specification, the *%%Document-Fonts* comment line is quite important, should the illustration be imported by a publishing application.

The *%%EndProlog* comment shows where the logo script begins.

```
%!PS-Adobe-1.0
%%Title: switch2.ps
%%DocumentFonts: Helvetica-Bold
%%BoundingBox: 100 350 500 500
%%Creator: Peter
%%CreationDate: 5 Sept 1989
%%EndComments

/Bold /Helvetica-Bold findfont 100 scalefont def
/strich { 500 -500 rlineto } def
/sprung { -500 496 rmoveto } def
/Background { gsave
             150 { strich sprung } repeat
             stroke grestore } def
/strich2 { 500 -480 rlineto } def
/sprung2 { -500 475.9 rmoveto } def
/Background2 { gsave
             150 { strich2 sprung2 } repeat
             stroke grestore } def

%%EndProlog
```

```
100 350 translate

newpath 0 0 moveto 0 150 lineto
400 150 lineto 400 0 lineto
closepath clip     % cutting out the whole logo

gsave
   newpath
   0 0 moveto
   8 setflat      % impact on performance
   Bold setfont (SWITCH) true charpath clip

   newpath
   0 550 moveto
   .4 setlinewidth
   Background2
grestore

0 74 moveto
Bold setfont (SWITCH) show

newpath
0 550 moveto
0.4 setlinewidth
Background

showpage
%%Trailer
```

See Figure 39.

SWITCH logo version 3

If the designer wishes we can modify the spacing between the letters. The keyword is 'Kerning'. Theoretically, PostScript offers an operator, namely *kshow*. But in relation with *charpath clip* this operator isn't very useful. Therefore, we are programming the kerning 'manually', by doing a small relative motion to the left between each pair of letters.

The corrections amount, for instance, to 10 points to the left between S and W, 5 points to the left between W and I, and 7 points to the left between C and H. The *kshow* operator is used in the last logo version only.

Figure 39 SWITCH logo, version 2

The structuring comment lines – e.g. %%EndProlog – are provided again.

```
%!PS-Adobe-1.0
%%Title: switch3.ps
%%DocumentFonts: Helvetica-Bold
%%BoundingBox: 100 350 500 500
%%Creator: Peter
%%CreationDate: 5 Sept 1989
%%EndComments

/Bold /Helvetica-Bold findfont 100 scalefont def
/strich { 500 -500 rlineto } def
/sprung { -500 496 rmoveto } def
/Background { gsave
             150 { strich sprung } repeat
             stroke grestore } def

/strich2 { 500 -480 rlineto } def
/sprung2 { -500 475.9 rmoveto } def
/Background2 { gsave
              150 { strich2 sprung2 } repeat
              stroke grestore } def

%%EndProlog
```

```
100 350 translate

newpath 0 0 moveto 0 150 lineto
400 150 lineto 400 0 lineto
closepath clip    % cutting out the whole logo

gsave
   newpath
   0 0 moveto
   8 setflat
   Bold setfont
   (S) true charpath -10 0 rmoveto   % manually
   (W) true charpath -5 0 rmoveto    % modifying
   (I) true charpath -5 0 rmoveto    % the
   (T) true charpath -10 0 rmoveto   % inter letter
   (C) true charpath -7 0 rmoveto    % spacing
   (H) true charpath               % (kerning)
   clip
   newpath
   0 550 moveto
   .4 setlinewidth
   Background2
grestore

0 74 moveto
Bold setfont
  (S) show -10 0 rmoveto          % manually
  (W) show -5 0 rmoveto           % modifying
  (I) show -5 0 rmoveto           % the
  (T) show -10 0 rmoveto          % inter letter
  (C) show -7 0 rmoveto           % spacing
  (H) show                        % (kerning)

newpath
0 550 moveto
0.4 setlinewidth
Background

showpage
%%Trailer
```

See Figure 40.

Figure 40   SWITCH logo, version 3

SWITCH logo final version

We come to the final version of the PostScript program. The program is to be modified four times:

- The logo construction is packed into the *Signet* routine, which has the 'scaling factor' operand. Signet can be invoked e.g. by

      0.5 Signet

  Width and height are halved.

      Thus, the *%%EndProlog* comment marking the end of the definition section, is shifted.

- *CutWhole:* compared with the other versions, this version defines the *clip* path at the beginning of the program in a modified way. In the original size, the version 4 logo has a width of 375 typographical points = some 13.2 cm. The height amounts to 178 typographical points = some 6.2 cm.

- If we would scale down the logo, the spacing between the strokes of the pattern would become too small. Therefore, the spacing between the strokes of the pattern is made dependent on the scaling factor. The equation is:

$$spacing = 4 \left(1 + \frac{1 - factor}{influence} \right)$$

Here, *factor* = scaling factor, and *influence* is set to 1. In the original size of the logo, the pattern spacing amounts to 4 typographical points. Now this value is modified according to the equation. The example shows how to calculate with PostScript. The following arithmetic operators are used: *sub, div, add, mul.*

Concerning *Background* and *Background2,* the *repeat* loop specifies how many lines are stroked. If the spacing is 4, then

$$\frac{560}{4} = 140$$

lines are stroked; this is valid for the original size of the logo. In the case of a reduction of the logo size, you have less than 140 strokes, because the *spacing* variable is a bit bigger than 4. The *cvi* operator manages the result of the division to be converted to an integer number (ConVersion to Integer).

- Kerning: the *kshow* operator is used. It handles kerned pair letter-spacing adjusting the spacing between pairs of letters. See the *Kern* procedure.

Before invoking *Signet,* the origin of the coordinate system is translated *(translate).* In order to suppress the addition of the translations, we can encapsulate each logo by issuing the *gsave grestore* pair. As already mentioned, the Signet routine expects one operand. If you forget the operand, the PostScript interpreter will issue a *stackunderflow* error message.

```
%!PS-Adobe-1.0 EPS
%%Title: switch4.ps
%%DocumentFonts: Helvetica-Bold
%%BoundingBox: 80 100 360 360
%%Creator: Teddy and Peter
%%CreationDate: 5 Sept 1989
%%EndComments

/Signet {
/factor exch def    % scaling factor operand

/CutWhole { newpath 0 0 moveto 0 178 lineto
           375 178 lineto 375 0 lineto
           closepath clip } bind def

/spacing 4 1 1 factor sub 1 div add mul def
          % intra pattern spacing is
          % dependent on scaling factor

/Bold /Helvetica-Bold findfont 100 scalefont def
```

```
/strich { -178 178 rlineto } bind def
/sprung { 178 spacing add -178  rmoveto } bind def
/Background { gsave
             560 spacing div cvi { strich sprung }
                                                   repeat
             stroke grestore } bind def

/strich2 { -184 178 rlineto } bind def
/sprung2 { 184 spacing 1.040 mul add -178 rmoveto }
                                                   bind def
/Background2 { gsave
             560 spacing div cvi { strich2 sprung2 }
                                                   repeat
             stroke grestore } bind def

/Kern {{pop pop 0 rmoveto} exch kshow} bind def
                                              % kerning
%
factor factor scale
CutWhole        % cutting out the logo

gsave
   newpath
   09 15 moveto
   8 setflat
   Bold setfont
   (S) true charpath -10 0 rmoveto
   (W) true charpath -5 0 rmoveto
   (I) true charpath -5 0 rmoveto
   (T) true charpath -10 0 rmoveto
   (C) true charpath -7 0 rmoveto
   (H) true charpath
   clip                   % cutting out SWITCH

   newpath
   0 0 moveto
   .4 setlinewidth
   Background2
grestore

09 89 moveto
Bold setfont

-7 -10 -5 -5 -10 (SWITCH) Kern   % kerning
```

```
newpath
0 0 moveto
0.4 setlinewidth
Background

} bind def    % end of the logo definition

%%EndProlog

% calling up Signet in various sizes:
gsave
    80 240 translate
    0.66 Signet
grestore

gsave
    80 165 translate
    0.35 Signet
grestore

gsave
    80 100 translate
    0.25 Signet
grestore

gsave
    300 100 translate
    0.15 Signet
grestore

showpage
%%Trailer
```

See Figure 41.

Figure 41   SWITCH logo, final version

6.

Creating Illustrations on Mac and IBM PC

Let us first turn to the Adobe Illustrator. The Illustrator'88 program from Adobe is available for both the Macintosh and the IBM PC or PS/2 under MS Windows.

The Adobe Illustrator

An Illustrator document is an EPS file that consists basically of two parts:

1. The PostScript program that describes the illustration graphics. The illustration may be output onto any PostScript device.
2. The screen representation – a WYSIWYG approximation with a resolution of 72 pixel/inch.

The basic idea of Adobe Illustrator is that the user first reads a draft or a photograph into the personal computer with the help of a scanner. Then, the graphical display of the Macintosh or the IBM PC represents it as a digitized image. By using the tools offered by Adobe Illustrator, the pixel graphics (or raster graphics) are finally converted into line art or vector graphics. The technique resembles the tracing method. If the beginner has a template or draft he or she will be able to print satisfactory line work onto paper. For instance, the PC user may use TIFF or .PCX files as his or her templates. The illustration graphics may be refined by the user tracing lines and curves with the help of the mouse. In this context, the Bézier control points (BCP) of the cubic or smoothed curves are of special importance. The crucial PostScript operator is the *curveto* operator. The Adobe Illustrator user never actually contacts the PostScript program. The PostScript language code is generated by Adobe Illustrator, and not by the user.

The auto trace tool of Adobe Illustrator

On a mouse click, this Illustrator'88 tool encloses any closed bitmapped template with a Bézier curve. This way, scans are vectorized automatically and can save much work. The paths gained this way must be refined and postprocessed for perfect results.

The Illustrator version '88 also provides additional tools for the designer, such as the Freehand tool for drawing by hand and the Blend tool for merging two different paths.

Illustrator 1.93 supports the Adobe Type Manager (ATM).

From bitmaps to vector graphics

We distinguish between two notions:

Template   pixel graphics, bitmap, image, rasterized.

Art   line art, object-oriented, illustration, vectorized.

See Figures 42 and 43.

Figure 42 Fruit.template

The prologue of Illustrator'88

The complete prologue of the Adobe Illustrator version 1.1 is copied and commented in the paper *Adobe Illustrator Document Specifications* (Adobe Systems Inc., 1987) [7]. The paper edited by Adobe is 26 pages long. The Illustrator'88 prologue is larger still and therefore is not reprinted here.

Figure 43 Fruit.art

The EPSF head

The PostScript language code obeys the Structuring Conventions version 2.0. EPSF is
the abbreviation for *Encapsulated PostScript File* format, a format for describing
PostScript illustration graphics and images to be imported or embedded respectively.
The EPS File format simply consists of PostScript command lines and a number of additional comment lines for structuring the PostScript code. These comment lines are introduced by the two '%%' characters:

```
%!PS-Adobe-2.0 EPSF-1.2
%%Creator:
%%For:
%%Title:
%%CreationDate:
%%BoundingBox:
%%DocumentFonts:
```

This is the EPSF head. The vector graphics (art) optionally can be supplemented by a bitmapped representation at the screen (template). Here is the head of Illustrator'88:

```
%!PS-Adobe-2.0 EPSF-1.2
%%Creator: Adobe Illustrator 88(TM) 1.6
%%For: PC Information Center, Uni Zurich
%%Title: (Fruit.art)
%%CreationDate: (1.11.1988) (8:32 h)

%%DocumentProcSets: Adobe_packedarray 0 0
%%DocumentSuppliedProcSets: Adobe_packedarray 0 0
%%DocumentProcSets: Adobe_cmykcolor 0 0
%%DocumentSuppliedProcSets: Adobe_cmykcolor 0 0
%%DocumentProcSets: Adobe_cshow 0 0
%%DocumentSuppliedProcSets: Adobe_cshow 0 0
%%DocumentProcSets: Adobe_customcolor 0 0
%%DocumentSuppliedProcSets: Adobe_customcolor 0 0
%%DocumentProcSets: Adobe_Illustrator_881 0 0
%%DocumentSuppliedProcSets: Adobe_Illustrator_881 0 0
%%ColorUsage: Black&White
%%DocumentProcessColors: Black

%%DocumentFonts: Helvetica
```

This comment lists the fonts used by Illustrator. The correct PostScript names are specified, e.g. *Helvetica, Times-Bold, LetterGothic-Slanted, Palatino-Italic.* This allows the importing application to ensure the availability of the required fonts.

```
%%BoundingBox:12 134 621 421
```

BoundingBox: llx lly urx ury

specifies the rectangle within which all stroked or painted elements of the illustration are to be rendered. (llx,lly) and (urx,ury) are the coordinate positions of the lower left corner and the upper right corner of the box. The coordinate units are typographical points (1/72 inch). The value urx-llx must be an integer giving the maximum width of the illustration. The value ury-lly limits the height of the illustration, see *Positioning an illustration,* on page 142.

The BoundingBox values prove to be quite useful when embedding an illustration graphic in a document. This enables the embedding application to decide whether the illustration must be scaled down or enlarged.

```
%%TemplateBox:300 80 300 80
%%EndComments
```

If a bitmapped template also exists the BoundingBox of the template is specified.

EPS procedure sets

Now, the prologue of the Adobe Illustrator program begins (not reprinted here), refer to *Adobe Illustrator Document Specifications* (Adobe Systems Inc., 1987) [7]. The prologue may be composed of several *procedure sets,* each of which is an independent package of procedures appropriate for a specific task. The corresponding structure comments are *%%BeginProcSet* and *%%EndProcSet.* Example:

```
%%BeginProcSet:Adobe_cmykcolor 0 0
% cmykcolor Operators
   ...
   ...
%%EndProcSet
```

The graphics state of the Adobe Illustrator corresponds approximately to the graphics state of the PostScript interpreter (the coordinate system CTM, the current position, the current path, the font, the line width, the color, etc.). In addition, the Adobe Illustrator knows:

- A separate color for filling areas.
- A separate color for stroking lines.
- Additional font metric data (e.g. kerning: spacing between the letters 'W' and 'o' for instance).

The 'heart' of the prologue

Constructing paths: before a line can be rendered as a stroke, a path must have been constructed. All Illustrator path operators are based on the PostScript *moveto* (m = motion), *lineto* (l = line), and *curveto* (c,v,y = curves) operators. Probably, the most widely used Illustrator operator is the *c* operator with the Bézier control points (BCP) as operands. By using this operator, cubic or smoothed curves may be constructed, which are needed for representing natural objects, e.g. garlics in Figure 44.

The *%%EndProlog* comment (not listed here) marks the end of the prologue section and the beginning of the script section of the document.

The script of Adobe Illustrator

The script lists all elements of an illustration, e.g. paths and strings, in a systematic way. Thus, only higher operators are used that have been predefined in the Illustrator prologue. We distinguish between state elements and object elements.

You can think of PostScript graphics as object-oriented – as opposed to bitmapped graphics or rasterized images, because the elements of the graphics may be identified as single objects while in a bitmap no single objects are recognized, only pixels.

The following script was generated by Illustrator'88:

```
%%BeginSetup
Adobe_cmykcolor /initialize get exec
Adobe_cshow /initialize get exec
Adobe_customcolor /initialize get exec
Adobe_Illustrator881 /initialize get exec
%%EndSetup

0 O
0 g
0 R 0 G
1 i 0 J 0 j 0.27 w 4 M []0 d
```

Note the *%%BeginSetup* and *%%EndSetup* structuring comments.

```
%%Note: this code was generated by Illustrator'88
204.311 306.937 m
216.389 301.447 235.055 304.741 222.977 289.369 c
210.899 273.997 217.487 272.899 219.683 261.919 c
221.879 250.939 228.467 248.743 217.487 242.155 c
206.507 235.567 209.801 236.665 203.213 224.587 c
S
0.09 w
222.977 309.133 m
266.897 344.269 204.584 395.328 y
S
0.27 w
205.409 306.937 m
S
252.347 190.273 m
266.621 200.155 269.915 191.371 280.895 208.939 c
291.875 226.51 281.993 219.919 299.561 228.706 c
317.129 237.49 306.149 242.98 299.561 260.548 c
292.973 278.116 297.365 277.018 318.227 281.41 c
339.089 285.802 324.815 287.998 322.619 306.664 c
S
```

```
313.013 305.839 m
314.111 295.957 323.993 292.663 302.033 290.467 c
314.162 291.68 283.428 278.096 291.053 270.703 c
327.287 235.567 319.601 241.057 315.209 236.665 c
S
314.111 308.035 m
319.601 293.761 332.777 282.781 319.601 278.389 c
306.425 273.997 297.641 270.703 305.327 258.625 c
313.013 246.547 318.503 245.449 313.013 233.371 c
S
323.444 306.937 m
327.836 301.447 327.836 304.741 328.934 288.271 c
330.032 271.801 330.032 272.899 336.62 260.821 c
343.208 248.743 329.483 255.331 330.581 244.9 c
S
0.36 w
286.661 385.993 m
292.7 398.073 299.837 402.465 326.189 406.857 c
345.714 410.11 345.953 400.269 359.129 413.445 c
372.051 426.365 370.956 436.784 386.579 441.993 c
393.167 444.189 398.657 446.385 y
S

   . . . . .

%%Trailer
Adobe_Illustrator881 /terminate get exec
Adobe_customcolor /terminate get exec
Adobe_cshow /terminate get exec
Adobe_cmykcolor /terminate get exec
/#copies 2 def
showpage
```

The trailer section can be used to restore the environment to its original state at the end of a document.

The *showpage* operator has to be inserted by the user if the graphic illustration is going to be printed as an independent (non-embedded) document. We set the *#copies* variable to 2. Thus, the *showpage* operator will produce the graphics twice.

Due to the universality of PostScript, the EPS files generated by Adobe Illustrator can be embedded not only into Macintosh or PC documents, but also for instance into Page-maker documents under OS/2 or markup documents on the IBM mainframe (Advanced Function Printing).

Garlics as an Illustrator example

See Figure 44.

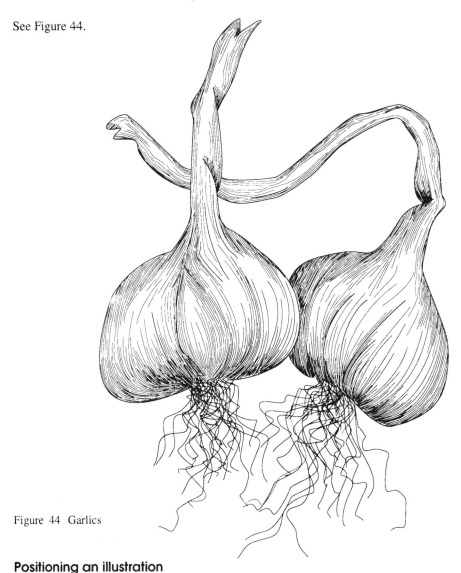

Figure 44 Garlics

Positioning an illustration

When you have generated a PostScript file and transferred it onto a personal computer, you may be disappointed because the printer attached to the PC outputs only a blank page. This may happen if the origin of an Illustrator document is not located at the lower left corner of the paper sheet, but in a different position. That can be corrected by using the *translate* operator.

With an Illustrator document, the origin of the coordinate system is normally located at the lower left position. However, the origin may have been shifted. In order to correct this you must specify the following *translate* operator:

```
llx neg lly neg translate
```

The values for *llx* and *lly* are taken from the BoundingBox specifications. After you have translated the illustration onto the position (0,0) of the new page, you can position it by issuing another *translate* operator:

```
nx ny translate
```

Where *nx* and *ny* are the coordinates of the new origin.

After having placed the illustration that way, a reduction or an enlargement may be required if only a certain area is available. You can do this with the help of the BoundingBox specifications:

```
nux nlx sub    % new width
urx llx sub    % width of BoundingBox
div            % proportion horizontal
nuy nly sub    % new height
ury lly sub    % height of BoundingBox
div            % proportion vertical
               % both x and y operands are on stack
scale          % scale down or enlarge
```

If for instance the BoundingBox has a width of 10 cm and the available area a width of 5 cm only, the proportion amounts to

$$\frac{5cm}{10cm} = 0.5$$

The illustration is scaled down by 50%. This is also valid for the vertical dimension (height).

Encapsulated PostScript for the IBM PC

The Macintosh user can generate the PostScript code in order to embed it on an IBM PC. The Encapsulated PostScript code is concerned, being always complete. Illustrator'88 can save an illustration in one of three ways *(save as):*

1. PostScript only (preview None)
2. Encapsulated PostScript (preview for Macintosh)
3. Encapsulated PostScript (preview for IBM PC)

See Figure 45.

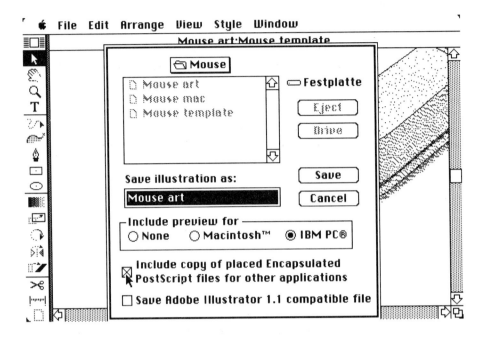

Figure 45   Generating an EPS file for the IBM PC

Clicking into the *preview for* ... button causes the generation of the so-called 'preview' file for the bitmapped representation at the screen – in addition to the generation of the PostScript language file.

The format of the bitmapped representation:

Macintosh   PICT format (QuickDraw)

IBM PC   Microsoft Windows MetaFile or TIFF (Tag Image File Format)

These formats are used for displaying a template at the screen only; the actual PostScript language file serves for producing the high-quality document.

It may be the case that the Illustrator document contains additional images in the EPS File format. Such images may have been produced for instance by programs such as ImageStudio, SmartArt, MacPerspective, Pixel Paint, Pro3D, Enabling 3D Draw, or Super3D and have been imported by using the *Place* option from the Illustrator File menu. In this event when saving, please don't forget to copy the additional EPS file too.

In order to do this click into the *Include copy of placed Encapsulated PostScript files for other applications* button.

Adobe Streamline

The conversion of bitmaps into line arts can be achieved by the *Streamline* program from Adobe too. With Adobe Streamline you can convert black and white images into reproduction-quality artwork in the EPS File format. The converted image may require fine-tuning once it is brought into your drawing program, but it beats coaxing along an autotrace tool. A typical application is creating and maintaining a database with company logos. Streamline is available on Mac and under MS Windows.

The prologue of a Streamline-generated EPS file contains the old Adobe Illustrator procedure set:

```
%!PS-Adobe-2.0 EPSF-1.2
%%Creator:Adobe Illustrator(TM) 1.1
%%For:Martin Heller
%%Title:streamline.eps
%%CreationDate:Fri Jan 26 13:45:13 1990

%%DocumentProcSets:Adobe_Streamline_1.1 0 0
%%DocumentSuppliedProcSets:Adobe_Streamline_1.1 0 0
%%DocumentFonts:
%%BoundingBox:0 0 576 720
%%TemplateBox:0 0 576 720
%%EndComments
%%BeginProcSet:Adobe_Illustrator_1.1 0 0
% Copyright (C) 1989 Adobe Systems Incorporated.
   ...
%%EndProlog
```

The script generated by Streamline corresponds to the script of Adobe Illustrator 1.1.

The Windows version of Adobe Streamline reads TIFF, compressed TIFF, PCX, and MacPaint input formats, and can produce output files in Adobe Illustrator Windows version, EPS and Micrografx Designer formats.

Micrografx Designer, GEM Artline, Corel Draw on the IBM PC

For the IBM PC users, there exist several alternatives to Illustrator and FreeHand. *Designer* of Micrografx is a Windows program able to import scanned bitmap graphics and retain the outlines and vectors. *Designer, GEM Artline, Corel Draw* and *Diagraph Windows* to date are the PC programs to compete with the Illustrator and FreeHand Mac programs. As well Designer and GEM Artline as Corel Draw and Diagraph Windows can convert scanned images into resolution-independent vector graphics or line art respectively. The advantage of the PC programs over the Mac programs is the symbol library. You can add symbols by simply clicking on single parts of a drawing and labeling these by number and name.

Formats supported for import/export

PC program	GEM	PCX	TIFF	CGM	WMF	HPGL	EPS*
Adobe Illustrator	X	X	X	-	X	X	X
GEM Artline	X	X	X	-	-	X	X
Corel Draw	-	X	X	X	X	X	X
M. Designer	-	X	X	X	X	X	X

GEM: .IMG, CGM: ISO format, WMF: MS Windows Metafile, HPGL: Hewlett-Packard

* Encapsulated PostScript Files: for export

The *Computer Graphics Metafile* (CGM) format and the GPI under OS/2 are competing with the EPSF format.

GEM Artline

Artline is fully integrated in GEM, therefore can be used in a comfortable way. It is an object-oriented program but can process pixel-oriented graphics as well. It displays pixel graphics in the background. The PCX, IMG, and TIFF file formats are readable.

Version 2.0 extends the first release of GEM Artline, by incorporating the color separation and auto tracing functions. The color separation allows you to create a PostScript file producing four color-separated films when processed on a Linotronic or Compugraphic recorder or another PostScript-compatible typesetter.

Designer version 2.0

The Micrografx Designer version 2.0 offers the following enhancements:

- Compatibility with the Presentation Manager of OS/2.
- Color fountains defined exactly by Pantone colors.
- Auto tracing as with Illustrator'88.
- Editing smoothed curves.
- Drawing smoothed curves by free hand.
- Color separations.

A Designer EPSF head

```
%!PS-Adobe-2.0  EPSF-1.2
%%Creator: C:\WINDOWS\WORK\ICU
%%Title: LOGO.EPS
%%CreationDate: Mar 28th 1990
%%BoundingBox: 7 576 362 789
%%DocumentFonts: (atend)
%%DocumentProcSets:MGXPS_2.1 0 0
%%DocumentSuppliedProcSets:MGXPS_2.1 0 0
%%Pages:(atend)
%%EndComments

%%BeginProcSet: MGXPS_2.1 0 0
   ...
```

Illustrations saved that way in the EPS File format may be exported into Xerox Ventura, PageMaker, or MS Word 5.0, etc.

Corel Draw

Corel Draw, operating under MS Windows and OS/2, offers the functions Bézier curves (smoothed or cubic curves), auto tracing, fountains and typefont effects. An EPS file generated by Corel Draw consists of two parts: the screen representation in the MS Windows Metafile format and the standard PostScript language file. The screen representation allows the display of the imported EPS file. This simplifies and speeds up the placing, scaling, and clipping of the graphics by any layout program.

If you have access to a PostScript printer, the EPSF format is mostly suited for exporting the graphics into a page layout or a word processing program. It is the best format because it contains the most information. If you read your EPS illustration into the page layout program it will be printed exactly as under Corel Draw. In addition, the size and position of the imported graphics may be modified by the layout program. In Page-Maker, Ventura Publisher, and Word 5.0, the illustration even may be clipped. Data about title, date, and author are inserted automatically. As expected, Corel Draw provides the bounding box of the graphics.

An EPS code generated by GEM Artline

The EPS code generated by GEM Artline is impressively simple. The Artline prologue gets along with a dozen rather simple definitions. The complete code consists of three parts:

1. The EPS head with the comment lines beginning '%%'.
2. The definitions.
3. The script with the line art (vector graphics).

```
%!PS-Adobe-2.0 EPSF-1.2
%%Creator: GEM Artline by CCP
%%Title: Bi-Centennial
%%Comment:
%%CreationDate: 03/07/89, 12:42:48
%%BoundingBox:  97.7 17.0 532.9 760.3
%%EndComments


%
% Copyright (C) CCP Development GmbH 1988.
% All rights reserved.
% GEM and GEM Artline are Trademarks of Digital
Research
%
```

Specifying the BoundingBox information is quite important in the EPS head (see above) to communicate the illustration size to the embedding application.

```
/#copies 1 def

/g  { setgray } bind def
/i  { newpath moveto } bind def
/l  { lineto } bind def
/m  { moveto } bind def
/c  { curveto } bind def
/f  { gsave eofill grestore } bind def
/r  { setrgbcolor } bind def          % colors
```

```
/s  { setlinewidth stroke } bind def
/cp { closepath } bind def
/sf { currentscreen                    % screen
      4 -2 roll pop 3 1 roll setscreen } bind def
/sa { currentscreen
      3  1 roll pop 3 1 roll setscreen } bind def
```

These definitions serve to construct abbreviations for the often used operators, such as:

g	changing the current gray scale
i	beginning a new path
l	constructing a line path
m	changing the current position
c	constructing a smoothed curve (cubic curve)
f	filling a closed path (area fill)
r	changing the current color
s	stroking a path
cp	closing a path
sf and sa	changing the screen of an output device

```
gsave
60 sf
474.7 631.5 i
478.2 628.0 l
478.8 625.0 479.1 621.3 480.8 618.9 c
483.5 614.8 487.9 613.6 491.8 612.3 c
518.1 603.2 l
516.8 620.4 510.6 626.2 498.0 623.1 c
497.1 625.7 496.2 628.6 495.2 631.4 c
504.1 633.7 510.4 631.2 515.7 621.3 c
517.9 617.0 519.5 612.0 520.1 606.7 c
520.7 600.1 521.1 600.2 523.2 594.1 c
520.7 595.0 l
520.5 588.7 520.5 578.1 514.3 576.4 c
507.8 574.5 502.9 583.8 500.1 590.0 c
499.2 584.5 497.6 579.4 492.7 578.8 c
486.4 578.3 481.1 584.1 478.3 590.7 c
472.2 604.5 475.1 616.2 474.7 631.5 c
```

```
499.7 601.8 m
500.1 597.6 500.8 593.8 502.9 590.5 c
505.0 587.2 508.1 584.8 511.5 584.7 c
517.0 584.5 517.9 589.8 518.1 595.3 c
499.7 601.8 l
514.1 556.7 m
515.8 558.4 517.4 559.6 519.5 560.7 c
520.9 558.3 522.3 555.9 523.5 553.3 c
521.7 552.0 519.9 550.6 518.1 549.3 c
516.6 551.7 515.3 554.1 514.1 556.7 c
cp f   % closing path and filling
489.9 523.0 i
489.7 525.9 489.7 528.7 489.7 531.5 c
489.7 546.7 l
493.9 543.5 l
493.9 520.3 l
489.9 523.0 l
cp f   % closing path and filling
482.2 473.8 i
479.8 474.9 l
476.5 482.4 473.8 490.3 473.5 499.0 c
472.9 510.7 478.1 518.7 487.6 518.5 c
502.9 518.3 515.9 506.8 520.5 488.3 c
522.6 480.1 522.7 472.0 517.9 465.4 c
514.8 467.2 511.7 468.9 508.5 470.5 c
507.7 473.4 l
513.6 472.9 518.5 474.4 518.5 483.6 c
518.5 489.1 516.1 494.4 513.0 498.1 c
508.5 503.8 502.2 506.8 495.9 508.3 c
488.2 510.3 477.2 509.2 476.7 496.2 c
476.3 488.3 479.5 480.7 482.2 473.8 c
cp f   % closing path and filling
490.0 456.5 i
   ...
525.1 31.2 525.7 31.8 525.6 32.6 c
525.6 33.4 525.0 33.7 524.3 33.7 c
523.9 33.7 523.8 33.7 523.8 33.2 c
523.8 31.5 l
0.040 0.040 0.040 r cp f
0.000 0.000 0.000 r .0 s
grestore
  showpage
```

According to the PostScript imaging model, a two-level procedure is followed:

1. Constructing a path.
2. Stroking the path or filling the closed path (stroke or area).

As the textbook explains it, the illustration is bracketed or capsulated by *gsave – grestore,* in order to preserve the graphics state of the main document. That way, an EPS file generated by GEM Artline may be embedded by PageMaker for instance, provided that the *showpage* operator is dummied.

The example

See Figure 46.

EPS files by Harvard Graphics

Harvard Graphics is a business graphics program that can generate Encapsulated PostScript files. This capability is documented by the following EPS head:

```
%!PS-Adobe-2.0 EPSF-1.2
%%Creator: Harvard Graphics
%%Title: communication research
%%BoundingBox: 60 190 540 720
%%Pages: 0
%%DocumentFonts: Helvetica Times-Roman Times-Italic
%%+ IntlHelvetica IntlTimes-Roman IntlTimes-Italic
%%DocumentSuppliedFonts: IntlHelvetica IntlTimes-Roman
%%+ IntlTimes-Italic
%%EndComments
```

The bounding box is declared, and the used fonts are listed. The font names prefixed by *Intl* refer to the reencoded fonts with the international character set (ä, ö, ü, é, è, à, ç, etc.).

```
/HGdict 30 dict def   % define local dictionary
HGdict begin %push dictionary onto dictionary stack
/s /stroke load def
/m /moveto load def
/l /lineto load def
/f {findfont exch scalefont setfont} bind def
```

Figure 46 Artline graphics in the EPS format (bi-centennial)

```
/10 {setlinewidth 0 setdash} bind def
/11 {s [20 80] 1 10} bind def
/12 {s [300 150] 1 10} bind def
/13 {s [] 30 10} bind def
/14 {s [] 1 10} bind def
/sn {stringwidth pop neg} bind def
/rj {sn 0 rmoveto} bind def
/cj {sn 2 div 0 rmoveto} bind def
```

Various operators are defined. These definitions are followed by a reencoding routine and the encoding vector which support the international character set (not reprinted here).

```
end   %pop HGdict off the dictionary stack
%%EndProlog
```

The *%%EndProlog* comment marks the end of the prologue section and the beginning of the script section of the graphic document.

Note the position of the *%%BeginSetup* and *%%EndSetup* comments:

```
%%BeginSetup
save   % saving state
HGdict begin
72 2400 div dup scale % scaling the coordinate system
1 setlinewidth 0 setlinecap 0 setlinejoin
[] 0 setdash 0 setgray 10 setmiterlimit

%%BeginFont: IntlHelvetica
/Helvetica  /IntlHelvetica spanvec ReEncodeSmall
%%EndFont

%%BeginFont: IntlTimes-Roman
/Times-Roman /IntlTimes-Roman spanvec ReEncodeSmall
%%EndFont

%%BeginFont: IntlTimes-Italic
/Times-Italic /IntlTimes-Italic spanvec ReEncodeSmall
%%EndFont
%%EndSetup
```

The *ReEncodeSmall* routine reencodes the fonts by using the *spanvec* encoding vector. The encoded fonts carry the *Intl* prefix in their names, stressing the international character set is supported.

The script describing the graphic illustration follows:

```
%%Page: one 1
newpath
2400 3000 translate    % translating the origin
14
s s 0.93 setgray
5929 3277 m
5929 4369 l 9672 4369 l 9672 3277 l 5929 3277 l eofill
s 0 setgray
5929 3277 s m
5929 4369 l 9672 4369 l 9672 3277 l 5929 3277 l
s s 0.93 setgray
9516 6709 m
9516 6715 l 9515 6743 l 9511 6770 l 9505 6797 l
9498 6824 l 9488 6851 l 9476 6878 l 9462 6904 l
9445 6930 l 9427 6956 l 9408 6982 l
    . . .
```

This script describes some line graphics by addressing the operators defined in the prologue section of the EPS file.

```
7800 3901 s m
(formelle und) cj
(formelle und) show
7800 3433 s m
(informelle Kontrolle) cj
(informelle Kontrolle) show
s end restore                  % restoring state
%%Trailer
```

An EPS file doesn't need to contain (but may contain) a showpage operator since that
operator is addressed by the including application. If an application such as MS Word
5.0 imports the EPS file it always takes the bounding box information as the 'truth'. The
placed illustration may be resized or clipped by MS Word, Word Perfect, PageMaker,
etc.

Mathematica on NeXT and Macintosh

Several representations of graphics are in common use by Mac and NeXT applications.
Wolfram Research describes the formats generated by Mathematica:

PostScript   PostScript representations are text-based and resolution
                               independent. PostScript graphics are used by high resolution
                               printers such as laser printers or typesetters, and by the

Mathematica kernel.

Encapsulated PostScript   This format is a PostScript-based representation that can easily be imported into non-PostScript documents by applications such as PageMaker, and Illustrator.

Embedded PostScript   This format is a screen representation in which PostScript is embedded in comment fields. Embedded PostScript graphics can be pasted into any application that is capable of using graphics.

Other screen representations

A bitmap representation is based on individual pixels in an image. Bitmaps are resolution dependent.

Each of these graphics representations has its advantages and drawbacks. The Mathematica Front End allows you to convert between them. Some sections of the User Manual cover ways to convert graphics from one file format to another.

The FreeHand alternative

There is competition. *FreeHand* is another program product and is sold by Aldus. As Illustrator does, it works with the features of PostScript. The FreeHand product is well suited for drawing from scratch for working with text logos, see Figure 47. FreeHand gives complete control over objects that have to be represented three-dimensionally.

In addition, the user can write his/her own PostScript programs for the output device in a special PostScript window: this window is selected by *PostScript fill* of the Fill menu. When you have drawn some closed paths you may define the filling pattern by entering a small PostScript program. The program example produces the 'cookie-cookie-cookie-cookie-cookie' background. Note the use of the *clip* operator which is very much like a cookie cutter.

Your own PostScript program:

```
/Roman /Palatino-Roman findfont 36 scalefont def
/str (cookie-cookie-cookie-cookie-cookie) def
/crlf
    { currentpoint 30 sub
    exch pop 0 exch moveto } def
/printstr { str show crlf } def
/Background
    { 25 { printstr } repeat } def
```

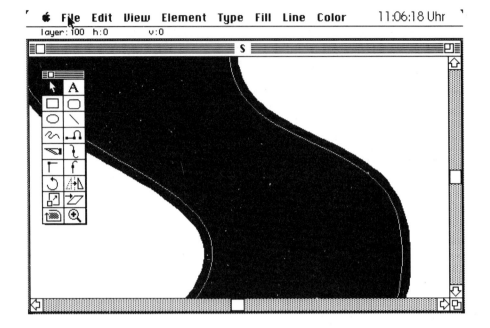

Figure 47 The Macintosh screen of FreeHand 2.0

```
clip

newpath 0 730 moveto
Roman setfont Background
```

As Illustrator'88 does, FreeHand supports color. FreeHand 2.0 also enables the user to produce color separations.

An EPSF document generated by FreeHand consists of two parts:

Print format   This file consists of the complete PostScript code.

Picture format   This is the bitmap for displaying a template at the screen of a Mac or an IBM PC.

An embedding application can display the bitmap at the screen (preview), while the PostScript program is used for printing. This mechanism of EPSF guarantees the high-quality output of the illustration, but enables the user to see and scale an approximation at the screen.

The object-oriented drawing program CricketDraw

CricketDraw is an object-oriented graphics program for production of illustration drawings and line art. It is available on Apple Macintosh.

This – quite old – program may interest you because it generates a *complete*
PostScript code, as do Illustrator'88 and GEM Artline; i.e. it uses its own prologue. The
PostScript file can be generated by clicking with the mouse on the *EPSF* (= Encapsulated
PostScript File) option under the menu *save as*.

The EPS file generated by CricketDraw consists of two parts: the so-called resource
fork and data fork. The PostScript language file in ASCII (data fork) is discussed later.

The other part (resource fork) contains a bitmapped format to be displayed at the
screen. In order to support the WYSIWYG concept (What You See Is What You Get),
the PostScript file may be supplemented by a bit-mapped screen representation. This
means, that the importing or embedding application can display the document at the
screen (preview facility) while using the PostScript program for printing or typesetting.
This mechanism ensures the high quality of the illustration, but enables the user to see
and to scale an approximation at the screen.

The versions 1.1 and 1.2 allow production of color separations for four-color printing.

The PostScript window

In a special PostScript window, the user may write his or her own PostScript programs.
In order to do so, click on the *Window Type: PostScript* button while opening a file.
Then under *Goodies,* CricketDraw 1.1 offers a PostScript help. Furthermore, the
PostScript programmer can use a library with PostScript language routines. While saving
a PostScript window the Macintosh displays the menu as shown in Figure 48.

The CricketDraw manual comments upon this: You can save the PostScript text file
in one of three ways:

Brief   Saves only the listed PostScript.

Complete   Saves the listed PostScript and the Cricket PostScript proce-
                       dures.

EPSF   Is needed by other applications.

If you wish to include the Cricket PostScript header, click on the *Complete* button. This
option needs to be selected if CricketDraw is not going to be used to download the file to
the printer – for example, if the file is being transmitted to a service bureau for typesetting.

Choose the *Complete* option, if the self-made PostScript language program is to be
printed at another location. Click on the *EPSF* button, if the PostScript program is to be
exported into another application, such as PageMaker.

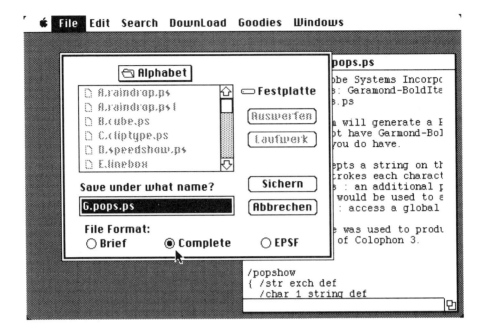

Figure 48   Saving the PostScript window

An EPS code generated by CricketDraw

An EPS code generated by a driver program is intended to be used by other applications. To the user therefore, such a code is not always easy on the eye.

In the manual, the CricketDraw prologue is called *Header*. The PostScript routines are named *Procedures*. The PostScript code obeys the Structuring Conventions version 2.0, as does the PostScript code of Adobe Illustrator. EPSF is the abbreviation for Encapsulated PostScript File format, a format for PostScript graphics and images to be imported. Essentially, the EPS File format consists of basic PostScript code and a number of comment lines that structure the PostScript code.

The three parts

The prologue of the CricketDraw version 1.1 consists of three parts:

1.   A procedure that alters the coordinate system: *fixcoordinates*

2.   Procedures that create paths, i.e. the object description:
     • *doarc* creates an elliptical arc

- *doroundrect* defines the dimensions of the rectangle and the shape of its curved corners
- *dobitmap* images a bitmap, in hexadecimal form, onto the drawing
- ...

3. Procedures that operate on paths:
    - *strokearrow* places an arrowhead at the beginning, ending, or both ends of a pre-viously defined path
    - *shadow* creates a shadow based on a previously defined path
    - *fountain* applies a linear, log, or radial fountain through a previously defined path at a specified angle
    - *pathtext* positions a string of text along a previously defined arbitrary path
    - *makeoutlinefont* creates a 'true' outline font based on any other font
    - ...

For reasons of space, only the beginning and the end of the prologue are reprinted here.

CricketDraw version 1.1

From release to release, the PostScript code generated by a software product becomes more complex and less easy on the eye.

```
%!PS-Adobe-2.0 EPSF-1.2
%%Creator:Cricket Draw 1.1
%%Title:diamon.eps
%%CreationDate:9/19/88    2:47 PM
%%BoundingBox:0 561 163 781
%%Pages:0
%%EndComments
/vmstate save def
[] settransfer
/$cricket 210 dict def
$cricket begin         % dictionary
```

The *begin* operator pushes the $cricket dictionary onto the dictionary stack.

```
1 -1 scale    57 -700  translate
```

This code converts from the coordinate system used by QuickDraw (upper left origin!) to the PostScript coordinate system.

```
2 setlinecap
/d /def load def
/b {bind d}bind d
/l {load d}b
```

```
/e /exch l
/x {e d}b
/C /closepath l
/CP /currentpoint l
/SH /show l
/g /gsave l
/G /grestore l
/i /if l
    . . .
```

Here, abbreviations for the PostScript operators often used by Cricket are predefined.

```
/ma {* +}b
/h {D * e D ma sqrt}d

systemdict D /setpacking known D
{/packstate currentpacking d D setpacking}i /pack? x
```

Older PostScript printers don't yet know the *setpacking* operator.

```
    . . .
    . . .
    . . .

/xreflect {[1 0 0 -1 0 0] concat} bdef
/yreflect {[-1 0 0 1 0 0] concat} bdef
```

Objects can be reflected, either horizontally or vertically in this way.

```
/shear
{/theshear exch sin def
[1 0 theshear 1 0 0] concat
}bdef
```

In this way, objects are sheared or slanted.

```
    . . .
/JoinProcs {jp}d
/fixcoordinates {fc}d
/doarc {a}d
/doroundrect {rr}d
/dograte {dg}d
/dorgrate {drg}d
```

```
/pathoffset {po}d
/pathtext {pt}d
/dostarburst {sb}d
/dobitmap {bm}d
```

Here, the procedures capable of constructing paths have been listed.

```
        . . .
        . . .
        . . .
    %%EndProlog
```

The *%%EndProlog* comment marks the end of the prologue section and the beginning of the script section of the document.

Procedures and operands

The *fixcoordinates* procedure to modify the coordinate system has the following operands:

1. Slope in degrees, 0 in the example.
2. 'true' or 'false' for vertical reflection, 1 in the example.
3. 'true' or 'false' for horizontal reflection, 1 in the example.
4. Rotation in degrees, 0 in the example.
5. Vertical position (center of the object), 109.500 in the example.
6. Horizontal position (center of the object), 80.932 in the example.

The origin of the coordinates lies in the center of the rhombus to be drawn (see Figure 49).

The *fountain* procedure calls up the PostScript *image* operator. This operator renders an image onto the current page. The routine draws 256 continuous gray scale values i.e. the pattern progressing continuousely. This means that each gray value is represented by 8 bits. The *fountain* routine has the following operands:

1. The angle of the pattern, 90 in the example.
2. The way of progressing (linear, logarithmic, radial), 1 in the example.
3. Gray scale begin, 0 (black) in the example.
4. Gray scale end, 1 (white) in the example.

The prologue also provides the 256-character long string for the progressing pattern shown. In the example, *fountainstring* contains all 256 possible 8-bit combinations; a printable subset of fountainstring: !"#$%&'()*+,-./0123456789:;<=>? etc.

The program script of CricketDraw

The script or main program comes after the prologue. In this example, a rhombus or diamond is drawn and filled with a pattern continuously progressing from black to white.
The horizontal and the vertical diameters amount to 2 times 80 points and 2 times 109
points respectively, these correspond to a width of 5.6 cm and a height of 7.7 cm. At the
end, the outlines are stroked by *stroke*.

```
%----- Begin Main Program -----%

gsave
0.000 1  1  0.000 80.932 109.500   fixcoordinates
newpath
0.000 -108.500  moveto
79.932 0.000 lineto
0.000 108.500 lineto
-79.932 0.000 lineto
closepath                 % rhombus
90  1 0 1 fountain        % filling
1.000 setlinewidth
0 setgray stroke          % strokes
grestore

%------ End Main Program ------%

end
vmstate restore

%%Trailer
%%Pages:1

showpage
```

The script isn't bracketed by *save/restore,* but by *gsave/grestore* only. However, this is
sufficient to ensure a clean graphics state at the end of the main program.

The *showpage* operator has to be inserted by the user if the illustration is going to be
printed as an independent (non-embedded) document.

The result generated by CricketDraw

See Figure 49.

Due to the universality of PostScript, the EPS files generated by CricketDraw can be
embedded not only into Macintosh or PC documents, but also, for instance, into Pagemaker documents under OS/2 or markup documents on the IBM mainframe (Advanced
Function Printing).

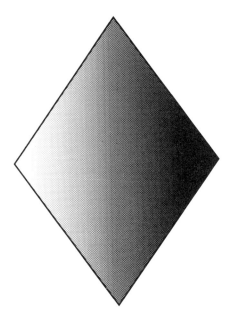

Figure 49 'Diamond' with gray scales (fountain)

CA-Cricket Stylist

CA-Cricket Stylist is the new, upgraded version of CricketDraw. Among the new features are full color support, an extended tool palette with full sets of Bézier drawing and transformation tools, and additional printing capabilities.

7.

Constructing Your Own Characters

First note that the Fontographer program is available on the Mac while Publishers Type-foundry runs on the IBM PC under MS Windows.

A designer can create graphics and refine images with Corel Draw or Adobe Illustrator; by using the Fontographer or Typefoundry, he/she additionally can construct his or her own fonttypes, see Figure 50. Fontographer and Typefoundry are similar in two respects:

1. Both programs help the user to convert templates or bitmaps into outline fonts.
2. Both programs generate a complete PostScript language code although the EPS File format isn't concerned (EPS Files describe illustrations, not typefaces).

Figure 50 A company logo

A font created by Fontographer or Typefoundry is downloaded onto a printer either temporarily (for the duration of a print job), permanently until power off or permanently onto the printer hard disk. The technical term is *font downloading*.

On the Macintosh, three independent display layers are shown for each character:

1. Foreground layer with the outlines.
2. Background layer with a template (if any).
3. Auxiliary layer with the base line and other guide lines.

The Fontographer, like the Adobe Illustrator or FreeHand, is a tool for the professional designer too. As opposed to bitmap fonts, the constructed character types are always printed out in the optimal resolution (important with the typesetter). Outline fonts are superior to the bitmap fonts because the outline fonts may be freely enlarged.

The Fontographer even allows you to modify characters of a Type 1 font (e.g. Helvetica). Practical experience shows that this is requested more often by the end user than the construction of completely new font designs. Since Fontographer version 3.0, the *original outlines* of the Adobe fonts and of other fonts are available if you have the *Metamorphosis* conversion utility program.

With version 2.4, any font *template* may be opened in two ways:

Composite
The characters of a standard font (e.g. Helvetica) should be supplied ready for add-on's, typically exotic or phonetic accents. A composite font is a reference to one or more existing PostScript fonts. When you attempt to print using a composite font, the definition of the original font must be in the printer.

Background
The characters of any font are shown only as templates at the screen. It is up to the user to click on the outline points (tracing).

Fontographer 3.0 can generate the PostScript file in three different shapes:

PostScript Macintosh
Choosing this option generates the standard PostScript font file. This font file can be used for both automatically downloadable fonts or fonts that are downloaded to the printer's hard disk. It is in this format that PostScript and the print driver recognize the file as a font. The characters generated in this file are in the compressed format. Compressed PostScript is the preferred form for generating fonts. Fontographer's compression scheme generates fonts which take up one-fifth the space, on average, of uncompressed fonts.

PostScript Compressed
Choosing this option generates the font file as an ASCII Text file. The font file is also compressed. The compressed form is generated as a string of numbers and letters which requires the font header to decipher.
Compressed character description example:

```
/n<97DD64574C90DC9EDCEE8A87DC...
EB7CD96B84D942D784D942D7EB...
6440D71D40D71DEB64AAEAFCF5>def
```

This option may be used for transferring Fontographer-generated fonts to non-Macintosh systems, such as the IBM PC. Such fonts can be downloaded to the printer from any type of computer system.

PostScript Uncompressed

This option is provided for PostScript programmers. It generates an ASCII text file with the standard PostScript definitions of the character. You may use this option to get the PostScript definition for all characters in the font. Under certain circumstances it may be appropriate to generate a small font in uncompressed format when the number of characters is small and the font must print as fast as possible.

Fontographer 3.0 even offers an autotracing tool. Instead of hand-tracing, you can paste PICT images into Fontographer's background layer and have Fontographer autotrace them for you.

Metamorphosis

Metamorphosis by *Altsys* is a utility designed to convert printer-resident PostScript fonts (Type 1, e.g. Helvetica) into editable outline formats. The software product can convert fonts using any Adobe PostScript printer, from the LaserWriter to professional typesetting machines. Fonts to be converted may be downloaded to the printer or resident in ROM. Metamorphosis essentially fetches the outline of the font selected from the printer and brings it back to the computer (at last).

During the process of conversion, Metamorphosis provides the option of creating editable outlines to be used in Fontographer to create Type 3 PostScript fonts (which can be used in any Macintosh application) or to create an EPS file useable in FreeHand and Illustrator, allowing artistic renderings from a typographical base. Extract from an EPS file generated by Metamorphosis, describing types:

```
u
%%Note:/five =53 117 681 554 0
117 681 m S
123.382523 716.463791 m
139.410812 716.463791 l
139.410812 713.248535 l
126.309845 704.514557
128.373367 705.138412 130.484879 705.138412 c
    ...
```

Metamorphosis uses the PostScript prologue of Adobe Illustrator 1.1.

A PostScript code generated by Fontographer

In this section we don't proceed from a standard font such as Helvetica, but use an example from the Altsys company which constructed the character types from scratch. The types are intended to represent the various components of two office chairs, see Figure 51.

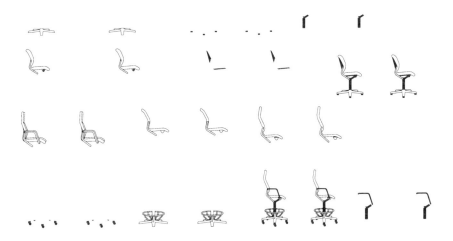

Figure 51 The components of a chair

The uncompressed PostScript code generated by Fontographer 3.0 corresponds to Fontographer 2.4 'PostScript text':

```
%!PS-Adobe-2.0
%%Title: Fontographer 2.4
%%FontName: My-Font
%%CreationDate: 9.12.1988 9:00:39 h
%%Creator: Earl
%%Pages: 0
%%EndComments
   ... Prologue ...
%%EndProlog
```

The end of the definition section generated by Fontographer is marked by the *%%End-Prolog* comment. After the prologue, the font dictionary follows, see chapter 5.3 in *PostScript Language, Reference Manual* (red book), Adobe Systems Inc., 1986 [2].

The Type 3 font dictionary:

```
/$KeyStrokeArt 19 dict def $KeyStrokeArt begin
/PaintType 0 def /FontType 3 def
/StrokeWidth 5 def
/FontBBox[-286 -309 2250 1089]def
/FontMatrix[0.000746 0 0 0.000746 0 0]def
/InvMtx[1341 0 0 1341 0 0]def
/CharDefs 257 dict def
/FontName (KeyStrokeArt) def
/BuildChar{AltRT6/BuildChar get exec}def
/FontInfo 3 dict def FontInfo begin
/UnderlinePosition -160 def
/UnderlineThickness 20 def end
/Encoding AltRT6
/MacVec get def CharDefs begin
/.notdef{500 0 setcharwidth} def
```

Type 3 fonts are unencrypted. Now, the definition of the characters begins...

```
% character a
/a {1644 0 126 -191 939 -7 Cache 500 -83 rmoveto
-278 -31 rlineto 0 18 rlineto
0 5 5 11 7 14 rcurveto
   ...
-32 -2 rlineto stroke } def

% character b
/b {1034 0 141 -196 936 -90 Cache 516 -162 rmoveto
50 0 rlineto 0 -29 rlineto -50 0 rlineto Cp
797 -95 rmoveto
50 -4 rlineto 0 -24 rlineto -50 0 rlineto Cp
230 -99 rmoveto
49 4 rlineto 0 -28 rlineto -49 0 rlineto
Cp Fill } def

% character c
/c {1034 0 251 -62 443 278 Cache 421 237 rmoveto
2 1 -6 2 -8 2 rcurveto -4 1 -10 5 -11 9 rcurveto
-6 14 rlineto -74 -43 rlineto -49 0
rlineto 18 -13 rlineto 6 -4 9 -16 3 -21 rcurveto
-2 -1 -7 -3 -10 -3 rcurveto -10 3 rlineto
0 -231 rlineto
59 0 rlineto 0 230 rlineto Cp
Fill } def
```

The predefined *Cache* operator specifies width and height of a character etc. Regarding the Type 1 fonts we speak of AFM (= Adobe Font Metrics), these are nothing other than the tables with the width and kerning data (width and kerning tables). For the PC, they also come in the PFM (Microsoft Windows) format.

Both *f* and *l* are combinations that use the *ShowInt* construct:

```
% combination f combines d, e, b, a, c.
/f {1000 0 141 -242 940 834 Cache gsave
[ 1 0 0 1 89 -172 ]concat 100 ShowInt
gsave [ 1 0 0 1 89 -170 ]concat 101 ShowInt
gsave [ 1 0 0 1 2 -2 ]concat 98 ShowInt
gsave [ 1 0 0 1 8 18 ]concat 97 ShowInt
gsave [ 1 0 0 1 241 43 ]concat
99 ShowInt Fill }def


% combination l combines m, j, k, i.
/l {901 0 106 -273 915 1137 Cache gsave
[ 0.902500 0 0 0.902500 196.939987 164.539993 ]concat
109 ShowInt    % combines m
gsave [ 0.902500 0 0 0.902500 0 -17.660000 ]concat
106 ShowInt    % combines j
gsave [ 0.902500 0 0 0.902500 127.252495 57.759998 ]
concat 107 ShowInt    % combines k
gsave [ 0.902500 0 0 0.902500 133.960007 112.289993 ]
concat 105 ShowInt Fill }def

end /EFN[]def
end % end of font dictionary

systemdict /currentpacking known {SavPak setpacking}if

/My-Font $KeyStrokeArt definefont pop
/My-Font findfont/EFN get AltRT6 begin{RF}forall end
```

The *definefont* operator registers *$KeyStrokeArt* as a font dictionary associated with *My-Font*.

In this example, Altsys completely constructed the following types: a, b, c, d, e, f, g, h, i, j, k, l, and m. Note, Fontographer uses for the character representation mainly the *rmoveto, rlineto, rcurveto* PostScript operators and at the end the PostScript routines defined in the prologue such as *ShowInt, Cp, Fill,* and *Eofill. ShowInt* is a quite special construct; it lets you combine different characters to a single character. See Figure 51.

EPS files and the Art Importer (Mac only)

On the base of EPS or PICT files, you can use the *Art Importer* (or the old *KeyMaster*) program by Altsys in order to construct company logos and assign these to keys of the keyboard. Each font created by the Art Importer is composed of 256 character slots, each of which corresponds to a character that can be typed from the keyboard. A slot can contain your logo, the shrunken head of your boss, the Eiffel Tower, or any graphic image you desire, see Figure 52.

Figure 52 Print example by MS Word with the Art Importer

Let's take your company logo. This should be available as artwork. The Art Importer gives you a way to import EPS artwork files from Aldus FreeHand, Adobe Illustrator, Streamline, or TypeStyler. These applications do save quality graphics or illustrations as Encapsulated PostScript Files. An EPS file usually consists of two parts, a screen representation (template) and the PostScript language code itself driving a laser printer or a typesetter. With regard to the Art Importer program, you could also use PICT files instead of EPS files. The Art Importer cannot, however, use PICT files which contain only bitmap images. But Color PICT2 drawings can now be imported with color intact.

Quite often when working with a word processing or layout program, it is desirable to use logos. At this point, the Art Importer program may be installed. It is simple therefore to have such EPS or PICT files imported and assigned to the keyboard characters. As already mentioned, the Art Importer can assign all 256 printable and non-printable character slots.

When you finally have chosen 'Save', the Art Importer operates as a font generator (The Art Importer comes from the Fontographer and Fontastic developers). Basically, two font files are generated:

1.   A bitmap font for displaying the logos at the screen, which has to be copied by the Font/DA Mover utility.
2.   A PostScript font defining the logo outlines on laser printers and typesetters (Autologic, Compugraphic, Linotype, Monotype, Scangraphic, Varityper, etc.). Simply put this font file into your system folder.

If you select this new font for instance in the MS Word application, the logos are displayed in the desired sizes at your screen, and the PostScript font downloaded automatically onto the printer reproduces the logos in the highest possible output quality (Figure 52).

Type manipulation software

TypeStyler enables the user arbitrarily to modify Type 1 fonts, and Type 3 fonts created by Fontographer, for instance to stretch and distort characters and their baselines (e.g. imitating the fish-eye perspective). The effects can be exported as files in the EPS format. Broderbund's TypeStyler lets you create sophisticated special effects with thousands of PostScript fonts.

Another type manipulation program is *LetraStudio,* which lets you create headlines, logos, signs, and other display type. It is now Type 1-compatible (like Metamorphosis).

Publishers Typefoundry on the IBM PC

For the IBM PC users, there is an alternative to Fontographer. *Typefoundry* by Z-soft is a Windows program using bitmap fonts to produce outlines. You can scan in logos and symbols and trace the outlines of the template at the screen with help of the mouse. Finally, PostScript types can be generated. Rotation, stretching, and distorting whole characters or single parts are possible.

Bitmap and outline editor

The two most important components of Publishers Typefoundry are the bitmap editor and the outline editor, by which the user produces and edits fonts in the vector format. The outline editor generates a PTF-ASCII format, that is translated into the PostScript language by a translator.

Once an outline font is constructed, it is easy to generate bitmap fonts automatically from this in various sizes. With very small point sizes (e.g. 7 points) only, it may be necessary to postprocess and refine a font produced in this way by a bitmap editor.

Downloading a font permanently with exitserver

If you want to download your font permanently onto the printer (permanently means until the next power-off) you must place in front of the generated code the following PostScript command:

```
serverdict begin 0 exitserver   % for PC fonts...
```

You quit the normal server loop by the *exitserver* operator and can store definitions and font dictionaries etc. permanently in the Virtual Memory of the printer. Beware: the number 0 in the example is the password of the printer. If the printer issues a *PasswordIncorrect* message, you specified a wrong password.

Type Studio

This is a PostScript font generator for the Ventura Publisher program.

8.

Digitizing Images with the Agfa Scanner

Together with an Agfa scanner, Agfa-Gevaert software supports the digital 'reading in' of images. The program is called MC View (on Macintosh) and PC View (on IBM PC). Images, photographs, drawings, etc. may be read into the computer. See Figure 53.

Figure 53 Landscape

Scanning is divided into scanning of line art and scanning of halftone images with gray scales.

A halftone image can be saved in different ways (in TIFF for instance); in this book, the Encapsulated PostScript File format (EPSF) is of main interest, although EPSF images need much disk space. The EPS File format consists of basic PostScript language code and a number of comment lines to structure the code. Consider the BoundingBox comment that reflects the size of an image. While saving, simply specify you wish the EPS File format. See Figure 54.

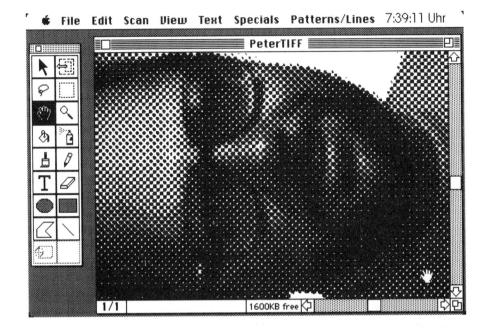

Figure 54 The MC View 2.0 screen

When the MC/PC View program saves an image in the PostScript format, this doesn't mean that you no longer have bitmap data. The bitmap data rather are enveloped by PostScript. In order to convert the bitmap data into line art it is necessary to use the tools of Adobe Illustrator, FreeHand, Corel Draw, or GEM Artline (tracing). Or you could vectorize the image by using *Vectorize Selection* of MC/PC View; see *Special Functions of MC/PC View* below. The automatic conversion of bitmap graphics into vector graphics could also be achieved by using the *Streamline* program by Adobe or the *OmniTrace* program by Caere. These programs generate EPS files.

Images in the EPS File format may have all their gray-scale data saved before screening. Such an image offers two advantages to the professional designer:

1.   Phototypesetter output to achieve high quality.
2.   You can enlarge the image in your page make-up program without incurring distortion from which screened images suffer due to size changes.

Thus, the screening of an image does not happen inside the scanner, but inside the printer.

The EPS code generated by MC/PC View

An image generally is coded hexadecimal. Every 8 bits are represented as hex. XX. For instance:

```
00          pixel with a gray scale of 0 (white)
5E          pixel with a gray scale of 94
91          pixel with a gray scale of 145
F0          pixel with a gray scale of 240
FF          pixel with a gray scale of 255 (black)
```

The example uses 8 bits to represent one pixel. This means, you are able to distinguish between 256 distinct gray scale values.

```
%!PS-Adobe-2.0 EPSF-1.2
%%BoundingBox:100 100 266.6 333.2
%%Creator:McView 1.1
%%Title: Peter
%%Creationdate: 25.01.1990  10:13 h
%%TemplateBox:0 0 0 0
%%DocumentProcSets:Adobe_Illustrator_1.1 0 0
%%EndComments

/W 463 def          % width in pixel
/H 648 def          % height in pixel
/resol 2000 def     % selected resolution: 200
/bresol 720 def     % typograph. points/inch: 72
/pix { bresol resol div mul} def
/W1 W pix def /H1 H pix def

gsave               % capsulate

100 100 translate % origin
W1 H1 scale
```

The whole image consists of 463 times 648 pixels. The pixel also is called 'pel' (picture element).

```
/trfunc       % function for settransfer:
{{/A1 1.3 def /B1 0 def
/A2 0.3 def /B2 0.7 def
dup .7 gt {A2 mul B2 add}
{A1 mul B1 add} ifelse }} bind def
```

```
% settransfer with LaserWriter only:
statusdict begin product (LaserWriter) eq
product (LaserWriter Plus) eq or
currenttransfer cvlit length 0 eq and
            {trfunc settransfer} if end
```

The *settransfer* operator allows correction of gray values to compensate for non-linear gray-level response in an output device, and in the human eye. The transfer function may also be redefined to produce specific effects, such as enhancing or reducing contrast in a sampled image.

```
% 45-degree screen:
100 45
{abs exch abs 2 copy add 1 gt
{1 sub dup mul exch 1 sub dup mul add 1 sub}
{dup mul exch dup mul add 1 exch sub} ifelse}
                                    setscreen
```

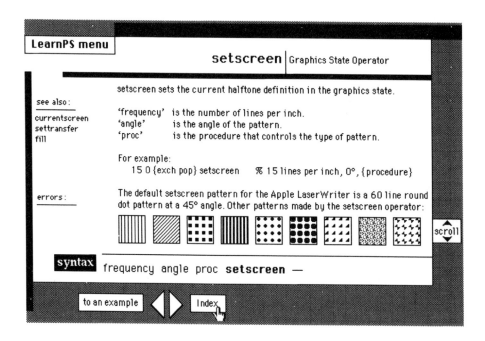

Figure 55 setscreen operator

ing technique to approximate the desired results. The halftone pattern or screen is under the control of the PostScript program which may execute the *setscreen* operator to establish a new screen. See Figure 55.

The PostScript image operator

This operator renders an image onto the current page.

```
/pstr W string def % string for half a scan line
/doimage
{W H 8 [W 0 0 H neg 0 H]
{currentfile pstr readhexstring pop}
                         image } def

% operands of image:
%     width, height, number of bits/pixel,
%     [matrix], {procedure}
```

The *image* operator has the following operands: *width in pixel, height in pixel, number of bits/pixel, matrix, procedure*. The PostScript interpreter 'thinks' of each image having its own coordinate system. Usually, the matrix consists of the following six values: *[width 0 0 -height 0 height]*. This matrix indicates, that the image was scanned from top to bottom.

The *image* operator executes the *currentfile pstr readhexstring pop* procedure again and again until all image data is available. *readhexstring* reads half a scan line from the current file and saves it into the *pstr* string variable.

readhexstring discards all non-hexadecimal characters, therefore all characters except '0' to '9' and 'A' to 'F', such as the blank and 'newline' characters, are discarded. And the *pop* operator destroys a useless object pushed by *readhexstring* onto the operand stack.

```
doimage
2727272727272327232727272727272327272727
2327272727272727272727272B27272727272727
2B272727272727272B2F2F2727272B2B2B2B2B2B
272727272B2B2B2B2B2F2F2B2B272B2B2B2B272B
2B272B2B2B272B2B2B2B27272B2727272B2B2B2B
2B2B2B2B2B2B2B2B2B2B2B2B2B2B2F2B2B2B2B2B2B
2B2B2B2F2F2B2F2F2F2F2F2F2F2F2F2F2B2F2F2F
2F2F372F2B2B2B2B2B2B2B27272B2B2B2B2B2B2B
2B2B27272727272727272B272B2B232323232323
23232323272B272B2B2B2B2F2F33332F2F372F2F
```

```
2B2B2F2F3333333333373333373B3B3B33333737
37373B3737373333333337333737373733737373737
373733372F3737373737373333373733337373737
373337333337373333333333333333333333333333
3333332F33332F332F332F333333333333333333
332F33332F33332F332F333333332F2F3333332F
2F2F2F2F2F2F2F2F2F2F2F2F2F2B2F2F2F2F2B2B2F
2F2B2F2B2B2F2B2F2B2B2B2B2B2B2B2B2B2B2B2B
2B2B2B2B2B272B2B2B2F2B2B2B2B2B272B2B2B27
2B2B2B27272727272727272727272727272727
27272727272727272727272727272727272727272B
2727272727272B27272727272727272727232727
27272727272727272727272B2F33D7DFEFFBFFFBFB
FFF7FF    % first scan line
27272727272727232723272727272727232727272723
27272727272727272727272727272B2B2B2727272727
27272727272727272B2B2B272727272B2B2B2B2B
272727272B2B272B2B2B2F2B2B2B2B2B2B2B2B2F
2F2B2B2B2B2B2B2B2B272B2B272B27272B27272B2B
2B2B2B2B2B2F2B2F2B2B2B2B2B2B2B2B2B2B2F2B
2F2B2F2F2F2F2F2F2F2F2F2F2F2F2F2F2F2B2F2F2F
2F2F2F2B2B2B2B2F2F2F2B27272B2B2F2F2B272B
2F2F272727272B2B272727B372F2F272723232323
1F1F231F2327272B2B2F2B2B2F33332F2F2F2F2F
2F2B2B2B3333333733373333373B3B3B37373333
3737372F37373737333343737373737373737373737
3737373F373F3737333737333337333337373337
3737373737373733333333333333333333333333
3333333333333332F332F333333333333333333
2F3333333333332F2F333333332F2F33332F2F33
332F2F2F2F2F2F2F2F2F2F2F2F2F2B2B2F2F2B2B
2F2F2B2B2F2F2B2B2B2B2B2B2B2B2B2B2F2B2B2B
2B2B2B2B2B2B2B2B2B2B2B2B2B2B2B272B2B2B27
2B2B2B272B272727272B27272727272727272727
27272727272B27272727272727272727272327272B
272727272727272727272727272727272727272727
272723272727272727272B2F33DBDFEFFFFFF7FB
FBFBFF    % second scan line
```

```
        . . .
        . . .
        . . .
777777636B736777736F6B73776F636B6F776B73
7B6F6F7B736B6F6F6F6B7F7B777777777B838377
777F837B7B837B777373737B7373777F7B776F77
6F7773776F6F7776F776B737B7B7B777F838B83
8F8F7B7F8B8B8F778B8383838B7F77838F878387
87878B8B837B8F877F7783837F7F8F87837B877B
6F737B7B7B736B83877B6B6B7B87737B7F77776B
7B7F7B6773637367776F735F735B5F63776B576B
6B63636F6B676B6B736B636B737B677B777B6B6F
6F6F636B676F6F776F73737B675F676F6F636B6B
736B6F776F777B5F6F7377736F736B776F6F6B77
6777777B736F6777776F6F737B7377776F6F6F6F
737B7B7B777F777F7F7B7B7B7373737B7B7B7383
77777B7B7B6B6F7B736B6F736F7783777777777B
777F776F7773777377837B877B7F838383878783
7F8B876F7F877F8787736F837783837F7F838377
83877F7B77777773736B636F737F7B877F7B7B7F
6B7F877373878B8F8F83777F837B7F7777838793
7F7F7B77777F73737 6F7783A7A38F7B87877787
8F7B8F877B938F737B8F7F6B6F6F735F63676F63
6B675F6F7B776B6F636F6377737F676F73677787
7F6F736F6F7367676B57534F4F47433F474F4F53
5F5F575F67736B6B6B6F6B7773736F6B6B676F73
A3D7F3   % this was the last scan line

grestore % capsulate
showpage
%%Trailer
```

MC/PC View envelops the *image* operator by a procedure named *doimage*. The entire image is encapsulated by *gsave* and *grestore*. The *showpage* operator finally outputs the current page.

Due to the universality of PostScript, the EPS files generated by MC/PC View can be embedded not only into Macintosh or PC documents, but also, for instance, into Page-maker documents under OS/2 or markup documents on the IBM mainframe (Advanced Function Printing). See Chapter 4 and Chapter 11.

A hint

The general painting and drawing programs on the Macintosh such as MacPaint and MacDraw save the template in the Paint or PICT format respectively. These formats may simply be converted into EPSF by carrying out following actions:

1.   Let MC View read the Paint or PICT file in.
2.   Save the template in the EPS File format.

Now, you have your preferred format suited for images (not line art) to be exported and embedded.

On the IBM PC, the user can apply a similar trick and convert various graphics formats into EPSF.

Special functions of MC/PC View

Among the special functions of MC and PC View there are functions that request a high computing power of the scanner, because calculations inside the set of all scanned points are performed. The 'Vectorize Selection' function belongs to these special functions. Here, the marked area is vectorized, i.e. the View program looks at every scanned point and its environment and tries to recognize line paths. These paths are represented as vectors. In contrast to the auto trace tool of Adobe Illustrator, MC/PC View processes an entire marked area, which may take rather a long time, corresponding to the size of the area. Finally, the vectors can be saved in the EPS File format according to Illustrator'88 (or saved in a non-PostScript format).

Example of an Illustrator code generated by MC/PC View:

```
%!PS-Adobe-2.0 EPSF-1.2
%%Creator:Adobe Illustrator(TM) and McView1.0
%%Title:View.art
%%Creation Date: 9.9.1989  15:40 h
%%BoundingBox:50 50 72 62
%%TemplateBox:0 0 0 0
%%DocumentProcSets:Adobe_Illustrator_1.1 0 0
%%EndComments
  . . .
 Prologue of Illustrator'88 ...
  . . .
```

```
%%Note: McView1.0
0.404 g
50.2 50.2 m
54.6 50.2 67.5 50.2 71.8 50.2 C
71.8 52.5 71.8 59.5 71.8 61.8 C
67.5 61.8 54.6 61.8 50.2 61.8 C
50.2 59.5 50.2 52.5 50.2 50.2 C
f
0.361 g
50.2 50.2 m
52.8 50.2 69.1 50.2 71.8 50.2 C
71.8 50.6 71.8 61.6 71.8 61.8 C
69.2 61.8 53.0 61.8 50.2 61.8 C
50.2 61.5 50.2 50.4 50.2 50.2 C
f
0.290 g
50.2 50.2 m
50.8 50.2 55.0 49.7 55.5 50.5 c
55.6 50.7 55.9 51.3 56.0 51.4 C
56.1 51.3 56.6 50.9 56.7 50.7 C
56.8 50.9 56.8 51.3 57.0 51.4 c
57.0 51.5 57.3 51.4 57.4 51.4 C
57.7 51.3 58.6 50.9 58.9 50.7 c
  ...
```

Other software products also use this method and try to convert a bitmapped image into the Illustrator-PostScript format, for instance the Adobe Streamline program (on Mac and under MS Windows).

9.

Learning the PostScript Language

Testing PostScript programs with Lasertalk

The Lasertalk software enables the Macintosh user and the PC user to test his or her PostScript programs easily. It was designed to provide all the tools necessary for both novice and experienced PostScript programmers to develop, maintain, and execute PostScript programs. In order to do so, a PostScript printer attached to the AppleTalk or attached serially must be exclusively available to the user. The Macintosh or personal computer is permanently connected with the printer controller, and a dialog occurs with the PostScript interpreter. The user may immediately react to messages from the printer.

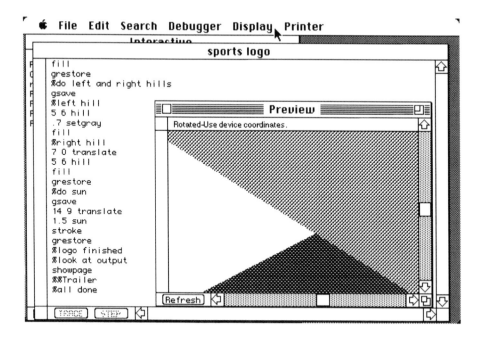

Figure 56 Lasertalk windows

A preview window gives an on-screen view of the PostScript page, exactly as it exists inside the PostScript printer. However the resolution of the display isn't the same as that of the page printer. A page printer usually outputs to a resolution four times higher. See Figure 56.

Dictionary Browser

Lasertalk gives you quick access to all unprotected PostScript dictionaries and font dictionaries. You can quickly inspect loaded fonts or look up a dictionary definition. At the University of Zurich, the *copypage* operator for instance was redefined. Lasertalk communicates:

```
/copypage
        {--gsave----showpage----grestore--}
```

PostScript dictionary handling is one of the most important areas of PostScript processing. All PostScript font and operator functions are performed by using dictionaries.

In addition, PostScript operator descriptions, excerpted from the PostScript Language Reference manual are available online.

Status Window

A user definable operand stack and status display, updated after each line is sent to the printer, is shown. If you wish, you may clear the operand stack, hence delete the current contents. Controlling the stack and a constant knowledge of the contents is a mandatory precondition for writing good PostScript programs.

Debugger

After you have opened a PostScript file, you are able to trace or step through a program or portion of PostScript code from the Edit/Debugger window. In this mode, you send your program, a line at a time, to the printer for execution. You may set break points or stop points respectively. Such break points have to be placed before the *showpage* operator in order to omit the output onto paper. Then you click on *Trace* in the debugger menu.

Lasertalk thus offers a number of tools to make the life of the PostScript programmer easier. Lasertalk supports the MultiFinder on the Mac, and on the personal computer, Lasertalk operates under Microsoft Windows.

PostShow for learning and testing

PostShow is a PostScript compatible interpreter by *Lincoln & Co.* that displays the
PostScript code graphically at the Macintosh screen. You enter the operators in one window, and the result is displayed in another. PostShow consists of the *LincPage* interpreter. In contrast to LaserTalk, a PostScript printer is not required. You can see the
PostScript graphic without having a PS printer. Programming errors are discovered and
monitored immediately.

Learning the PostScript language with LearnPS

Have you ever heard of HyperCard applications on the Macintosh? LearnPS is a *Hyper-
Card* stack that helps you to learn the PostScript language. LearnPS has two parts, the
LearnPS stack (see Figure 57) and the HelpPS stack (Figure 59).

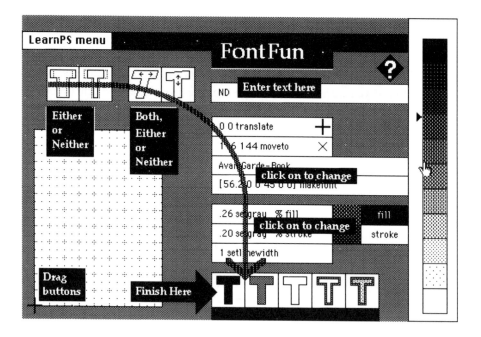

Figure 57 LearnPS with FontFun

The Macintosh and NeXT versions of LearnPS are developed by *John F. Sherman* at
the Notre Dame University in Indiana 46556, USA.

The LearnPS stack

The LearnPS stack consists of four basic parts: FontFun, ExamplesPS, the TryYourOwn card, and an introduction in PostScript (tutorial). *FontFun* tempts the student to transform a PostScript font in various ways. FontFun lets you make a number of decisions on placing type on a page. These decisions can include position, a transformation of its matrix, its value and/or the width of its outline.

ExamplesPS offers to the Macintosh user a library of PostScript language program examples, such as the following program with the *rand* operator, see Figure 58.

Random numbers

```
%!PS-Adobe-1.0
%%Creator: John F. Sherman
%%DocumentFonts: Helvetica
%%Title: random.ps
%%EndComments
% commented 16 Sept 1988/vo

/number {rand exch mod} def   % random numbers
/gray {100 number cvr .01 mul .1 add} def

/Hel /Helvetica findfont 18 scalefont def
/Hell /Helvetica findfont 36 scalefont def
/Helll /Helvetica findfont 72 scalefont def

/text {350 number 450 number moveto Hel setfont
       (Gutenberg) show} def
/textt {300 number 425 number moveto Hell setfont
        (Gutenberg) show} def
/texttt {250 number 400 number moveto Helll setfont
         (Gutenberg) true charpath stroke} def
%%EndProlog

8499583 srand         % starting random generator
100 150 translate
% 20 0 { exch pop } setscreen
```

```
% now we place randomly:
25 {gray setgray 100 {text} repeat } repeat
                    % with random gray scales
0 setgray 25 {textt} repeat
1 setgray 5 {texttt} repeat
showpage
%%Trailer
```

Figure 58 Gutenberg and the random generator

What is the purpose of the *rand* operator in this example? This operator gives us the random numbers that are first divided by 350 or 450 etc. in the *text, textt,* and *texttt* routines. The *mod* operator, addressed in *number,* gives back the modulo of the division. These remainder values are intended to position the 'Gutenberg' string somewhere on the paper sheet *(moveto)*. The gray scales too are set randomly. The *gray* variable accepts values between 0.1 and 1.1 and serves as operand to *setgray*.

With the help of *srand* we pass over a starting point to the random generator. We print the 18-point string 2500 times (two-five-zero-zero), the string in 36 points 25 times, and the string in outline characters five times.

The *TryYourOwn* card provides a text editor and a downloading program to the LearnPS user.

Finally, the tutorial gives a basic insight into the language. The topics: Drawing Squares and Lines, Drawing Circles and Arcs, Drawing Curves (very clear), PostScript and Type, etc.

The HelpPS stack

The second LearnPS component, the HelpPS stack, contains a list of all PostScript operators and their definitions (corresponding to the *PostScript Language, Reference Manual* (red book), Adobe Systems Inc., 1986 [2]). There are links to uses of operators in ExamplesPS. The first card of the HelpPS stack is the index card, see Figure 59.

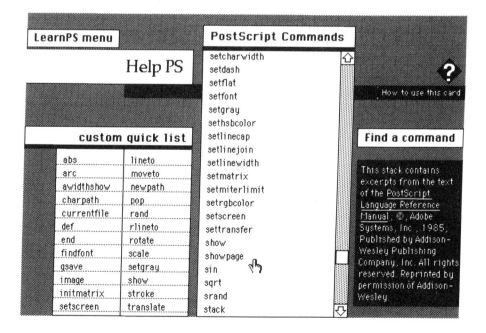

Figure 59 HelpPS

10.

Interpreter in the Printer or Computer

A PostScript interpreter, residing inside either a printer or a workstation, consumes and processes the PostScript language programs. Usually, we define a PostScript printer as an output device *with a built-in PostScript interpreter.* Exactly, we speak of a PostScript printer as of a high-performance controller with a built-in print engine. An exception is represented by publishing systems with a PostScript interpreter implemented on a PC adapter board (e.g. JetScript, Conodesk) or on the IBM mainframe (see *The PostScript Interpreter on the IBM Mainframe,* on page 192).

Hence, we distinguish between:

1.   The PostScript interpreter located in the printer, i.e. in the Apple LaserWriter or the QMS ColorScript.
2.   The PostScript interpreter located in the computer system or workstation, e.g. in the IBM PC or the NeXT computer.

In the first case, the communication of a PostScript printer to the external world happens:

*   Via the serial interface (RS232/422).
*   Via the Centronics interface (parallel input).
*   Via LocalTalk (formerly AppleTalk).
*   Or via Ethernet (TCP/IP).

The host or personal computer at the other end of the communication sends PostScript language programs or data intended to be processed by the PostScript interpreter to the printer. The communication goes in both directions. On the one hand, the printer receives programs and data, on the other hand, it sends messages back to the host computer. These messages for instance may have been generated by the PostScript *print* operator or by the error handling.

In the second case, a video or channel cable provides fast communication between computer and print engine. In the first case, the printer usually operates in a network.

Serial communication with the IBM PC

There are two ways of serially connecting a PostScript printer to the IBM PC. (For the parallel connection, see next page.)

XON/XOFF flow control

At your personal computer, key-in the following DOS commands:

```
MODE COM1:9600,n,8,1
MODE LPT1:=COM1:
```

That way, the serial port 1 of the personal computer is used for the communication. However, this isn't sufficient to ensure the flow control by XON/XOFF. That is up to the application programs.

'Data Terminal Ready' flow control

The availability of the DTR flow control simplifies the connection of a PostScript printer (e.g. LaserWriter Plus) to an IBM PC.

```
MODE COM1:9600,n,8,1,p
MODE LPT1:=COM1:
```

And the printer is initialized as follows:

```
%!PS LaserWriter Plus, QMS PS800, Qume or ...
0 serverdict begin exitserver   % password
statusdict begin
% serial 9600 bit/s, parity none, flow control DTR
  25 9600 7 setsccbatch
end
```

The number 0 represents the printer password.

Checking the sccbatch options

By downloading the following program, you may instruct the page printer to print out the options number (number from 0 to 7).

```
%!PS LaserWriter Plus, QMS PS800, Qume or ...
/Helvetica findfont 14 scalefont setfont
30 500 moveto
(The options number for the 25-pin connection
is  ) show
statusdict begin 25 sccbatch 10 string cvs show
pop showpage
```

The 'scc' stands for *Serial Communication Controller*. The *sccbatch* operator pushes the current speed (bit/s) and the options number (parity and flow control mode) on the operand stack. The computing center at the University of Zurich recommends its IBM PC users to set the options number to 3 (with XON/XOFF) or 7 (with DTR). For the LaserWriter II option numbers, please refer to the *LaserWriter II User Guide*.

Parallel input (Centronics)

Printers from *Agfa, AST, Canon, Hewlett-Packard, Kyocera, NEC, Olivetti, QMS, Qume, Texas Instruments, Unisys* and many others have a parallel interface.

The parallel interface is equipped with 36 pins. The signal pin assignments supported through this connector are:

```
1      Data Strobe
2-9    Data 1-8
10     Acknowledge
11     Busy
12     Paper Error
13     Select
14     Ground
19-29  Twisted Pair Ground
31     Iprime (Active low)
32     Fault (Active low)
```

The Centronics interface can be connected with the parallel port of the IBM PC. In contrast to the serial communication, the parallel input does not recognize any communication parameter. The Centronics interface receives 8-bit data without parity only, and it doesn't recognize either the XON or XOFF special character. The flow control is performed by the busy signal (separate wire).

The communication goes in the one way direction from the personal computer to the Centronics interface. However, the printer sends back error or *print* messages over the serial interface.

Checking the parallel input

In order to test a parallel connection, key-in the following DOS commands at your personal computer:

```
COPY CON LPT1:
showpage Control-D Control-Z
```

If the connection and the printer behave well, the printer will output a blank paper sheet.

LocalTalk and AppleTalk

In this book the notion *AppleTalk* is used synonymously with *LocalTalk*.

LocalTalk is a small local area network for connecting Macintosh PCs and printers. Some PostScript printers and typesetters (e.g. Apple LaserWriter, Linotype Series 100, QMS ColorScript) have a switch which allows manual switching to AppleTalk. Connecting a printer requires that you use a LocalTalk connector box.

While the printer is attached to LocalTalk, it listens for a connection request from a Macintosh PC. The printer server then executes a job using that connection as its source. Any error messages or other output produced by the *print* operator are sent back to the host over the same connection.

When the PostScript interpreter reaches end-of-file, the printer sends a matching end-of-file indication back to the host Mac, terminates the current job, and starts a new one. While the PostScript printer is busy with one connection, any further connection requests are refused. This causes the requesting hosts to queue and wait for the printer server to become free. The next request chosen is the one that has waited the longest.

It is possible to connect more than one page printer to the same LocalTalk network.

Font downloader

If you have attached any PostScript device to your AppleTalk net, then the *SendPS* print procedure allows you to send PostScript file (graphics, your own fonts, etc.) onto the printer. The setting of the communication and the permanent parameters is possible too by using *SendPS*.

Version 2.0 of SendPS provides some support for the PostScript structure comment conventions. In particular, it recognizes and expands the following comments:

%%IncludeFile: filename
> includes the named file in-line.

%%ExecuteFile: filename
> works like %%IncludeFile, except that it assumes that the included file is an executable EPS file that should be isolated from the rest of the code. The program actually brackets the file with save/restore when it is included.

%%IncludeFont: fontname
> includes the named font.

%%IncludeProcSet: name version revision
> treats the file in much the same way that %%IncludeFile does.

An alternative to SendPS is the *Adobe Font Downloader* program. This program allows a PostScript font to be downloaded either into the printer memory or onto the disk inside the printer. In addition, the printer state and the available fonts in the printer (font directory) may be interrogated. See Figure 60.

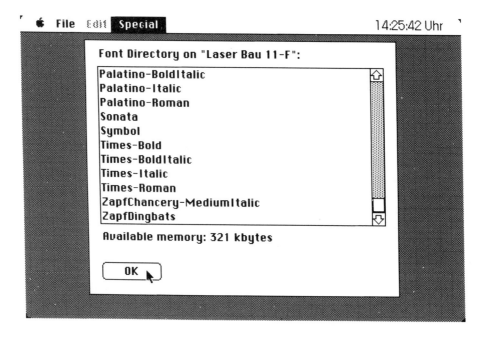

Figure 60   Font downloader: listing the font directory

Two font downloaders are provided with all Adobe PC-format fonts:

- A command line driven version for the parallel (LPT) port.
- A menu-driven version for the serial (COM) port.

Another alternative is the Apple LaserWriter Font Utility.

The PostScript interpreter on the IBM mainframe

The IBM Publishing Systems *PostScript Interpreter for Advanced Function Printing* (AFP) is a program that translates PostScript page description files into data files for IBM advanced function printers (see Figure 61). The program runs in the VM/CMS and MVS environments. The files you can process using the PostScript interpreter should have a filetype of *PS, EPS,* or *LISTPS.* The character set can be either ASCII or EBCDIC. The PostScript interpreter reads the entire file as either ASCII or EBCDIC characters based

Figure 61 PostScript interpreter: another effect

on the format of the first two characters of the file. The PostScript files are usually created on a personal computer (see Figure 61).

The 'Advanced Function Printing' IBM printers

When you process a PostScript file with the PostScript interpreter, you can print the
resulting file on one of several IBM printers. The PostScript interpreter produces a
'Composed Document Printing Facility (CDPF) image file' for printing on the IBM
4250/II ElectroCompositor. The interpreter also produces PSEG3820 files for printing on
any of the following:

- IBM 3812 Page Printer.
- IBM 3820 Page Printer.
- IBM 3827 Page Printer.
- IBM 3835 Page Printer.

Calling up the PostScript interpreter

You can use the PostScript interpreter to translate files in one of two modes: in the batch
mode or in the interactive mode. In the batch mode, the following panel is displayed:

```
===  Publishing System - PostScript Interpreter for  ===
                   Advanced Function Printing

               5688-104 Copyright 1988 IBM Corporation
             Portions Copyright Adobe Systems Incorporated

Option===>


                          Main Menu

      1 Create LIST File

      2 Create PSEG File

      3 Install PostScript Typeface


PF1 = Help   PF4 = Exit
```

Create LIST File   Use this option to translate a PS, EPS, or LISTPS file to a 4250 file. The PostScript interpreter brings in a data file and checks the first two characters of the file you specified to see whether the file is in ASCII or EBCDIC format. The first two characters should be '%!' for the PostScript interpreter to read the file properly.

Create PSEG File   Use this option to create a file for to be embedded in a document. The IBM manual SC34-5082 speaks of a *page segment*.

Install PostScript Typeface

Use this option to install an additional PostScript typeface.

PostScript interpreters in the IBM PC

By mid-1989, the following PostScript boards for the personal computer were on offer:

- Conodesk 6000 from Conographic Corp.
- PageStyler from Destiny Technology Corp.
- EiconScript Card from Eicon Technology Corp.
- PS-388 Accelerator from Princeton Publishing Labs Inc.
- JetScript from QMS or Hewlett-Packard.
- PC Publisher Kit Series II from Imagen or QMS.

By installing such a board in the personal computer, Hewlett-Packard's LaserJet or the Brother HL8 printer may be upgraded to a PostScript device. With the exception of JetScript all boards are PostScript clones. But Conographic has received confirmation of Adobe-compatibility.

DP-Tek LaserPort PS 600 produces some of the best output available with a LaserJet, equalled only by the latest LaserMaster LX6 boards.

DCA IrmaPrint

Digital Communications Associates (DCA), the manufacturer of the Irma card for attaching the personal computer to the IBM host, develops the Irma2Print converter software. The software translates IBM's SAA printer language called IPDS into PostScript. This enables host users to output onto PC PostScript printers which also reduces the host's workload. It is interesting that DCA concentrates on PostScript instead on the PCL LaserJet standard by Hewlett-Packard.

11.

EPSF Specification by Adobe

The author and publisher are grateful to Adobe Systems Inc. who gave permission for the EPSF specification (version 2.0) to be included in this book.

This document specifies the format required for import of Encapsulated PostScript (EPS) Files into an application. This specification suggests a standard for importing PostScript files in all environments, and contains specific information about both the Apple Macintosh and MS-DOS environments. This format conforms to Adobe Systems' PostScript Document Structuring Conventions, Version 2.0.

The rules that should be followed in creating importable PostScript files are a subset of the structuring conventions proposed by Adobe Systems Incorporated; refer to the *PostScript Language Reference Manual,* Appendix C, and PostScript Document Structuring Conventions, Version 2.0, available from Adobe Systems. Files must also be 'well-behaved' in their use of certain PostScript operators, manipulations of the graphics state, and manipulation of the PostScript interpreter's stacks and any global dictionaries. These conventions are designed to allow cooperative sharing of files between many systems using PostScript.

Fundamentally, an Encapsulated PostScript file is merely a standard PostScript language file with a bitmap screen preview included optionally in the format. The purpose of an EPS file is to be included into other document makeup systems as an illustration, and the screen representation is intended to aid in page composition. The bitmap is normally discarded when printing, and the PostScript language segment of the file is used instead. Typically any manipulation of the screen image that is performed by the user (such as scaling, translating, or rotation on screen) should be tracked by the page layout application and an appropriate transformation should precede the encapsulated PostScript when it is sent to the printer.

EPS file format guidelines

An EPS file should conform to at least Version 2.0 of the Adobe Document Structuring Conventions. This does not explicitly require any of the structuring comments to be employed, but if used, they should be in accordance with that specification. Additionally, an EPS file is required to contain the *%%BoundingBox* comment, and is required to be 'well-behaved' (see below). An EPS file may optionally contain a bitmap image suitable for WYSIWYG screen display, as discussed herein.

The structure of an EPS file is marked by PostScript comments, according to the *PostScript Document Structuring Conventions*. These are covered briefly here for reference. Structuring comment lines must begin with '%!' or '%%' and terminate with a *newline* (either return or linefeed) character. EPS file conventions require that a comment line be no longer than 256 bytes. A comment line may be continued by beginning the continuation line with '%%+'. The EPS file should begin with a 'header' of structuring comments, as specified in the PostScript Structuring Conventions.

Required participation

In order to support Encapsulated PostScript files effectively, some cooperation is required on the parts of those who produce EPS files and those who use EPS files (typically by including them into other documents).

When producing EPS files

There are certain required comments and several recommended ones that must be provided in the EPS file. These are detailed in the next section. The file must also be a single page (not a multi-page) document and must be a *conforming* PostScript document. Conformance requirements are mostly detailed here, but for the full specification, please refer to the *Document Structuring Conventions* from Adobe Systems (1989) [4].

When reading and using EPS files

When including an EPS file into your document, you should basically think of that piece of code as having been generated by your program. After all, this is what all programs (and users) who encounter your print file will think. In particular, you must find out enough about the file to intelligently make it part of your document. The only tricky part of this relates to font usage. This is also the most difficult part of this specification to understand. Basically, you just have to figure out what the requirements of the illustration are and incorporate them into your own requirements (pass them downstream). Then all issues of font management are essentially the same as they were before you included the illustration (and are beyond the scope of this document).

As long as you don't remove relevant information from a file, and as long as you update your global view of font usage and resource requirements to reflect those that you just imported, the rest is fairly easy. The intent behind the EPS specification, in fact, is to make the most of cooperation between producers and consumers of PostScript language files so that neither has to do much, but the combined advantage is great.

Required comments

The first comment in the header (and the first line in the file) should be the version comment:

```
%!PS-Adobe-2.0 EPSF-2.0
```

This indicates to an application that the PostScript file conforms to this standard. The version number following the word 'Adobe-' indicates the level of adherence to the standard PostScript Document Structuring Conventions. The version number following the word 'EPSF' indicates the level of EPSF-specific comments.

The following comment must be present in the header; if it is not present then an importing application may issue an error message and abort the import:

```
%%BoundingBox: LLx LLy URx URy
```

The values are in the PostScript default user coordinate system, in points (1/72 of an inch, or 2.835 mm), with the origin at the lower left corner. The bounding box must be expressed in default user coordinate space. This seems to be a big question among implementors of this specification. Regardless of the coordinate system in which your application operates, here is a foolproof of determining the correct bounding box: *print* the page, get out a point ruler, and *measure* first to the lower left corner, then to the upper right corner, using the lower-left corner of the physical paper as your origin. This works because it measures the end result (the marks on the page), and none of the computation matters.

Optional comments

The following header comments are strongly recommended in EPS files. They provide extra information about the file that can be used to identify it on-screen or when printing.

```
%%Title: included_document_title
%%Creator: creator_name
%%CreationDate: date_and_time
```

The *%%Creator, %%Title,* and *%%CreationDate* comments may be used by an application or spooler to provide human-readable information about a document, or to display
the file name and creator on the screen if no bitmapped screen representation was included in the EPS file.

```
%%EndComments
```

This comment indicates an explicit end to the header comments, as specified in the structuring conventions.

How to use these comments (philosophy)

All of the comments in EPS files provide information of some sort or another. Exactly
how you use this information is up to you, but you are encouraged not to reduce the
amount of information in a file (when you import it or include it, for example) by remov-
ing or altering comments. In general, the comments tell you what fonts and files are
used, and where. Not everybody cares about these things, but if you do care, then the
information is available.

The whole issue of Encapsulated PostScript files is that they are 'final form' print
files that may be far from the printer that they will actually be imaged on. If they have
specific needs, particularly in terms of font usage, these needs must be carefully pre-
served and passed on downstream, and the program that actually prints the composite
document must take pains to make sure the fonts are available at print time.

Any piece of software that generates PostScript language code is potentially both a
consumer and a producer of Encapsulated PostScript files. It is probably best not to think
that you are at either end of the chain. In particular, if you import an Encapsulated
PostScript file, integrate it into your document somehow, and then go to print your document, you are responsible for reading and understanding any of the font needs of the EPS
file you imported. These should then be reflected in your *own* font usage comments. If
the illustration on page 3 uses the Bodoni font but the rest of your document is set in
Times, suddenly your document now also uses the Bodoni font (you included the illustration, after all). This should be reflected in the outermost *%%DocumentFonts* comments
and any other appropriate ones.

Font management comments

If fonts are used, the following two comments (which are defined in Version 2.0 of the
PostScript Document Structuring Conventions) should be included in the header of the
EPS file. The *%%IncludeFont* and *%%Begin/%%EndFont* comments should be
thought of as inverses of one another. That is, if you encounter an *%%IncludeFont* comment and actually include a font file at that point, you should enclose the font in
%%BeginFont and *%%EndFont* comments. Conversely, if you see fit to remove a font
from a print file (one that presumably had been delimited with comments), you should
always replace it with an *%%IncludeFont* comment rather than completely stripping it.
This guarantees the reversibility of your actions.

```
%%DocumentFonts: font1 font2 ....
%%+ font3 font4
```

The *%%DocumentFonts* comment provides a full list of all fonts used by the file. Font names should refer to *non-reencoded* printer font names and should be the valid PostScript language names (without the leading slashes). An application that imports an EPS file should be responsible for satisfying these fonts needs, or at least updating its own *%%DocumentFonts* list to reflect any new fonts.

```
%%DocumentNeededFonts: font1 font2 ....
```

The *%%DocumentNeededFonts* comment lists all fonts that are to be included at specific points within the EPS file as a result of the *%%IncludeFont* comment. These fonts must also be listed in the *%%DocumentFonts* comment, but an application may or may not pre-load these at the beginning of the job. The responsibility should be taken, however, by any program that thinks it is actually printing the file, to make sure the fonts requested will be available when the file is printed. This may mean that the individual *%%Include-Font* comments may be satisfied and the fonts placed in-line, or they may simply be ignored, if the fonts are determined to be already on the printer. As a third possibility, there may be enough memory to download all the fonts in front of the job and avoid processing the individual requests. This *%%DocumentNeededFonts* comment provides foreshadowing of the *%%IncludeFont* comments to follow, to give printing managers enough information to make these choices intelligently.

```
%%IncludeFont: fontname
```

The *%%IncludeFont* comment signals to an application that the specific font is to be loaded at that precise location in the file. It is analogous to the familiar *#include* syntax in the C language. An application should load the specified font regardless of whether the same font has been loaded already by other preceding *%%IncludeFont* comments, since the font may be embedded within a PostScript save and restore construct. However, if the font is determined to be available prior to the entire included EPS file (for instance, it may be in ROM on the printer or might have been downloaded prior to the entire print job) the *%%IncludeFont* comment may be ignored by printing manager software.

When an application satisfies an *%%IncludeFont* request, it should *always* bracket the font itself with the *%%BeginFont* and *%%EndFont* comments.

A font that is wholly contained, defined, and used within the EPS file (a downloaded font) should be noted in the *%%DocumentFonts* comment but not the *%%Document-NeededFonts* comment. The font should follow conventions listed in the PostScript Document Structuring Conventions in order to retain full compatibility with print spoolers.

```
%%BeginFont: fontname
%%EndFont
```

The *%%BeginFont* and *%%EndFont* comments bracket an included downloadable font. The fontname is the simple PostScript language name for the font. These fonts may be stripped from the included file if they are determined to be available (but should be replaced by an *%%IncludeFont* comment).

File management comments

```
%%IncludeFile: filename
```

This comment, which can occur only in the body of an EPS file, allows a separate file to be inserted at any point within the EPS file. The file might not be searched for or inserted until printing actually occurs, so user care is required to ensure its availability. If it is used, the *%%DocumentFiles* comment should be used as well. See the Structuring Conventions for more information.

```
%%BeginFile: filename
%%EndFile
```

The *%%BeginFile* and *%%EndFile* comments bracket an included file. They are the 'inverse' of the *%%IncludeFile* comment. The filename is evaluated in the context of the local file system. These files may *not* be stripped from the included file at print time, because they undoubtedly contain executable code. However, they may be temporarily removed, or 'factored out' to save space during storage. They should always be replaced by the *%%IncludeFile* comment.

Color comments

```
%%DocumentProcessColors: keyword keyword ...
```

This comment marks the use of process colors within the document. Process colors are defined to be *cyan, magenta, yellow,* and *black.* These four colors are indicated in this comment by the keywords *Cyan, Magenta, Yellow,* and *Black.* This comment is used primarily when producing color separations. The *(atend)* convention is allowed.

```
%%DocumentCustomColors: name name ...
```

This indicates the use of custom colors within a document. These colors are arbitrarily named by an application, and their CMYK or RGB approximations are provided through the *%%CMYKCustomColor* or *%%RGBCustomColor* comments within the body of the document. The names are specified to be any arbitrary PostScript language string except (Process Cyan), (Process Magenta), (Process Yellow), and (Process Black), which need to be reserved for custom color implementation by applications. The *(atend)* specification is permitted.

```
%%BeginProcessColor: keyword
%%EndProcessColor
```

The keyword here is either *Cyan, Magenta, Yellow,* or *Black.* During color separation, the code between these comments should only be downloaded during the appropriate pass for that process color. Intelligent printing managers can save considerable time by omitting code within these bracketing comments on the other three separations. Extreme care must be taken by the document composition software to correctly control overprinting and 'knockouts' if these comments are employed, since the code may or may not actually be executed.

```
%%BeginCustomColor: keyword
%%EndCustomColor
```

The keyword here is any PostScript language string except (Process Cyan), (Process Magenta), (Process Yellow), and (Process Black). During color separation, the code between these comments should only be downloaded during the appropriate pass for that custom color. Intelligent printing managers can save considerable time by omitting code within these bracketing comments on the other three separations. Extreme care must be taken by the document composition software to correctly control overprinting and knockouts if these comments are employed, since the code may or may not be executed.

```
%%CMYKCustomColor: cyan magenta yellow black keyword
```

This provides an *approximation* to the custom color specified by *keyword*. The four components of cyan, magenta, yellow, and black must be specified as numbers from 0 to 1 representing the percentage of that process color. These numbers are exactly analogous to the arguments to the *setcmykcolor* PostScript language operator. The *keyword* follows the same custom color naming conventions for the *%%DocumentCustomColors* comment.

```
%%RGBCustomColor: red green blue keyword
```

This provides an *approximation* to the custom color specified by *keyword*. The three components of red, green, and blue must be specified as numbers from 0 to 1 representing the percentage of that process color. These numbers are exactly analogous to the arguments to the *setrgbcolor* PostScript language operator. The *keyword* follows the same custom color naming conventions for the *%%DocumentCustomColors* comment.

'Well-behaved' rules

An application should encapsulate the imported EPS PostScript code in a save/restore construct, which will allow all printer VM (memory) to be recovered and all graphics state restored. Since the code in the imported EPS file will be embedded within the PostScript that an application will generate for the current page, it is necessary that it obey the following rules, in order to keep from disrupting the enclosing document:

Operators to avoid

The following PostScript operators should not be included in a PostScript file for import; the result of executing any of these is not guaranteed:

- grestoreall
- initgraphics
- initmatrix
- initclip
- erasepage
- copypage
- banddevice
- framedevice
- nulldevice
- renderbands
- setpageparams
- note
- exitserver
- (setscreen)
- (settransfer)

The setscreen and settransfer operators

The *setscreen* operator is troublesome when one file is included within another. *setscreen* is a system-level command that is appropriate for changing the halftone machinery to compensate for marking engine tendencies, but when used for 'special effects' can cause problems. For EPS files, the *setscreen* and *settransfer* operators are permitted only under restricted terms.

The settransfer and setcolortransfer operators

The *settransfer* operator changes the gray-level and color response curves over the interval from 0 to 1. There are two basic uses of it: to invert an image (typically flipping blacks and whites, less often colors), or to adjust the response curve for a particular output device.

The best (and required) approach for using settransfer is to combine your function with the existing one. Here is the recommended way to do this:

```
{ dummy exec 1 exch sub }
dup 0 currenttransfer put settransfer
```

In this example, the desired transfer function is the code *1 exch sub*. The *dummy exec* essentially executes the existing transfer function before executing the new code. The name *dummy* is replaced by the actual procedure body from the existing transfer function through the *put* instruction. The result is conceptually equivalent to this:

```
{{ original proc } exec 1 exch sub } settransfer
```

This approach is better than 'concatenating' procedures because it does not require the existing transfer function to be duplicated (consuming memory).

The showpage operator

The showpage operator is permitted in EPS files primarily because it will be present in so many PostScript files. It is reasonable for an EPS file to use the *showpage* operator if needed (although it is not necessary if the file is truly exported to another document). It is the including applications responsibility to disable showpage if needed. The recommended method to accomplish this is as follows:

Temporarily disabling showpage

```
/BEGINEPSFILE { %def
  /EPSFsave save def
  0 setgray 0 setlinecap 1 setlinewidth 0 setlinejoin
  10 setmiterlimit [] 0 setdash
  newpath
  /showpage {} def
} bind def
/ENDEPSFILE { %def
  EPSFsave restore
} bind def

BEGINEPSFILE
  100 300 translate
  .5 .5 scale
  % include the EPS file here,
  % which may execute showpage with no effect

ENDEPSFILE   % restore state and continue
```

This method will only disable the *showpage* operator during the execution of the EPS file, and will restore the previous semantics of *showpage* afterward. It is the responsibility of the EPS file itself to avoid the operators listed in the previous section that might cause unexpected behavior when imported. They need not be redefined along with *showpage,* although it is permissible to do so.

Stacks and dictionaries

All the PostScript interpreter's stacks (including the dictionary stack) should be left in the state that they were in before the imported PostScript code was executed. This is normally the case for well-written PostScript language programs, and this is still the best way to keep unanticipated side-effects to a minimum. Please avoid unnecessary *clear* and *countdictstack 2 sub { end } repeat* cleanup techniques. If you have accidentally left something on one of the stacks, it is best to understand your program well enough to get rid of it, rather than issuing a wholesale cleanup instruction at the end, which will not only clear your operands from the stack, but perhaps will clear other objects as well.

It is recommended that the imported PostScript EPS file create its own dictionary instead of writing into whatever the current dictionary might be. Make sure that this dictionary is removed from the dictionary stack when through (using the PostScript *end* operator) to avoid the possibility of an *invalidrestore* error. Also, no global string bodies should be changed (with either *put* or *putinterval).*

If a special dictionary (like *statusdict)* is required in order for the imported PostScript language code to execute properly, then it should be included as part of the EPS file. However, it should be enclosed in very specific *%%BeginFeature* and *%%EndFeature* comments as specified in the Document Structuring Conventions. No dictionary should be assumed to be present in the printer, and fonts should be reencoded as needed by the EPS file itself.

The graphics state

When a PostScript language program is imported into the middle of another executing program, the state of the interpreter may not be exactly in its default state. The EPS file should assume that the graphics state is in its default state, even though it may not be. An importing application may choose to scale the coordinate system or to change the transfer function to change the behavior of the EPS file somewhat. If the EPS file makes assumptions about the graphics state (like the clipping path) or explicitly sets something it shouldn't (the transformation matrix), the results may not be what were expected.

The importing application is responsible for returning the color to be black, the current dash pattern, line endings, and other miscellaneous aspects of the graphics state to their default condition (as specified in the *PostScript Language Reference Manual* [2]). This can be done in either of two ways: the initial graphics state can be restored from variables, or the state can be explicitly set:

```
/BEGINEPSFILE { %def
   /EPSFsave save def
   0 setgray 0 setlinecap 1 setlinewidth 0 setlinejoin
   10 setmiterlimit [] 0 setdash
   newpath
   /showpage {} def
} bind def

/ENDEPSFILE { %def
   EPSFsave restore
} bind def
```

File types and file naming

Apple Macintosh files

The Macintosh file type for application-created PostScript files is EPSF. Files of type TEXT will also be allowed, so that users can create EPS files with standard editors, although the Structuring Conventions must still be strictly followed. A file of type EPSF should additionally contain a PICT resource in the resource fork of the file containing a screen representation of the PostScript code.

MS-DOS and PC-DOS files

The recommended file extension is .EPS. Other file extensions will also be allowed, but it will be assumed that these files are text-only files with no screen metafile included in them.

Other file systems

In general, the extension *.epsf* is the preferred way to name an EPS file, and *.epsi* for the interchange format. In systems where lower-case letters are not recognized or are not significant, all upper-case can be used.

Screen representation

The EPS file will usually have a graphic screen representation so that it can be manipulated and displayed on a workstation's screen prior to printing. The user may position, scale, crop or rotate this screen representation, and the composing software should keep track of these manipulations and reflect them in the PostScript that is ultimately sent to the PostScript printing device.

Apple Macintosh: PICT resource

A QuickDraw representation of the PostScript language file can be created and stored as a PICT in the resource fork of the file. It should be given resource number 256. If the PICT exists, the importing application may use it for screen display. If the *picframe* is transformed to PostScript coordinates, it should agree with the *%%BoundingBox* comment.

Given the size limitations on PICT images, this may not always agree for large illustrations. If there is a discrepancy, the *%%BoundingBox* always should be taken as the 'truth', since it accurately describes the area that will be imaged by the PostScript code itself. In this situation, applications *producing* the preview PICT must all take the same action so that the importing application knows what to do.

Since it is more important to have a reasonable facsimile of the image than it is to have any particular part of it be high quality, the PICT image should be *scaled* to fit within the constraints of the PICT format. That is, the picture will all be there (it will not be cropped), but it will actually be *smaller* than the real image. The importing application should then scale the PICT to a size which matches the bounding box as expressed in the *%%BoundingBox* comment.

DOS: Windows MetaFile or TIFF file

Either a Microsoft Windows MetaFile or a TIFF (Tag Image File Format) section can be included as the screen representation of an EPS file. The EPS file itself has a binary header added to the beginning that provides a sort of 'table of contents' to the file. This is necessary since there is not a second 'fork' within the file system as there is in the Macintosh file system.

It is always permissible to have a pure ASCII PostScript language file as an EPS file in the DOS environment, as long as it does not contain the preview section. The importing application should check the first three bytes of the file. If they match the header as shown below, the binary header should be expected. If the first two match '%!', it should be taken to be an ASCII PostScript language file.

EPS binary file header:

Header:	Bytes	Description
	0-3	Must be hex C5D0D3C6 (byte 0=C5)
	4-7	Byte position in file for start of PostScript code section.
	8-11	Byte length of PostScript section
	12-15	Byte position in file for start of Metafile screen representation.
	16-19	Byte length of Metafile section (PSize)
	20-23	Byte position of TIFF representation
	24-27	Byte length of TIFF section
	28-29	Checksum of header (XOR of bytes 0-27). Note: if Checksum is FFFF then it is to be ignored.

Note: It is assumed that either the MetaFile or the TIFF position and length fields are zero; that is, only one or the other of these two forms are included in the EPS file.

The MetaFile should follow the guidelines set forth by the Windows specification. In particular, it should not set the viewport or mapping mode, and it should set the window origin and extent. The application should scale the picture to fit within the *%%BoundingBox* comment specified in the PostScript language file.

Device-independent interchange format

This last screen representation is intended as an interchange format between widely varied systems. In particular, the bitmap preview section of the file is very simple and is represented as ASCII hexadecimal in order to be more easily transportable. This format is dubbed Encapsulated PostScript Interchange format, or *EPSI*.

This format wins no prizes for compactness, but it should be truly portable and requires no special code for decompressing or otherwise understanding the bitmap portion, other than the ability to understand hexadecimal notation.

It is expected that applications that support EPSF will gradually head toward supporting only two formats: the first is the 'native' format for the environment in which the application runs (where the preview section is Macintosh PICT or TIFF or Sun raster files or whatever); the second format should simply be this interchange format. Then files can be interchanged between widely varying systems without each having to know the preferred bitmap representation of the others.

```
%%BeginPreview: width height depth lines
%%EndPreview
```

These comments bracket the preview section of an EPS file in Interchange format (EPSI). The *width* and *height* fields provide the number of image samples (pixels) for the preview. The *depth* field provides how many bits of data are used to establish one sample pixel of the preview (1, 2, 4, or 8). An image which is 100 pixels wide will always have 100 in the *width* field, although the number of bytes of hexadecimal needed to build that line will vary if *depth* varies. The *lines* field tells how many lines of hexadecimal are contained in the preview, so that they may be easily skipped by an application that doesn't care. All the arguments are integers.

Some rules and guidelines for EPSI files

The following guidelines attempt to clarify a few basic assumptions about the EPSI format. It is intended to be extremely simple, since its purpose is interchange. No system should have to do much work to decipher one of these files, and the preview section is mostly just a convenience to begin with. This format is accordingly deliberately kept simple and option-free.

- The preview section must be after the header comment section but before the document prologue definitions. That is, it should immediately follow the *%%EndComments* line in the EPS file.

- In the preview section, bits of 0 are white, bits of 1 are black. Grayscale is not supported.

- The Preview image can be of *any* resolution. The size of the image is determined solely by its *bounding box,* and the preview data should be scaled to fit that rectangle. Thus, the *width* and *height* parameters from the image are *not* its measured dimensions, but simply describe the amount of data supplied for the preview. The dimensions are described only by the bounding rectangle.

- The hexadecimal lines must never exceed 255 bytes in length. In cases where the preview is very wide, the lines must be broken. The line breaks can be made at any even number of hex digits, since the dimensions of the finished preview are established by the *width, height,* and *depth* values.

- All non-hexadecimal characters should be ignored when collecting the data for the preview, including tabs, spaces, newlines, percent characters, and other stray ASCII characters. This is analogous to the PostScript language *readhexstring* operator.

- Each line of hexadecimal will begin with a percent sign (%). This makes the entire preview section into a PostScript language comment, so that the file can be printed without modification.

- If the *%%IncludeFile* or *%%BeginFile* / *%%EndFile* comments are ever used to extract the preview section from the EPS file, then the *lines* argument to the *%%BeginPreview* comment must be adjusted accordingly. The *lines* value specifies only the number of lines to *skip* if you're not the least bit interested.

- If the *width* of the image is not a multiple of 8 bits, the hexadecimal digits are padded out to the next highest multiple of 8 bits.

Example EPSI File:

Here is a sample file showing the EPS Interchange (EPSI) format. The preview section is expressed in user space and the correct comments are included. Remember that there are 8 bits to a byte, and that it requires 2 hexadecimal digits to represent one binary byte. Therefore the 80-pixel width of the image requires 20 bytes of hexadecimal data, which is

$$\frac{80}{8}\ 2$$

The PostScript language segment itself simply draws a box, as can be seen in the last few lines.

```
%!PS-Adobe-2.0 EPSF-2.0
%%BoundingBox: 0 0 80 24
%%Pages: 0
%%Creator: Glenn Reid
%%CreationDate: September 19, 1988
%%EndComments
%%BeginPreview: 80 24 1 24
% FFFFFFFFFFFFFFFFFFFF
% FFFFFFFFFFFFFFFFFFFF
% FFFFFFFFFFFFFFFFFFFF
% FFFFFFFFFFFFFFFFFFFF
% FFFFFFFFFFFFFFFFFFFF
% FFFFFFFFFFFFFFFFFFFF
% FFFFFFFFFFFFFFFFFFFF
% FFFFFFFFFFFFFFFFFFFF
% FF0000000000000000FF
% FF0000000000000000FF
% FF0000000000000000FF
% FF0000000000000000FF
% FF0000000000000000FF
% FF0000000000000000FF
% FF0000000000000000FF
% FF0000000000000000FF
% FFFFFFFFFFFFFFFFFFFF
% FFFFFFFFFFFFFFFFFFFF
% FFFFFFFFFFFFFFFFFFFF
% FFFFFFFFFFFFFFFFFFFF
% FFFFFFFFFFFFFFFFFFFF
% FFFFFFFFFFFFFFFFFFFF
% FFFFFFFFFFFFFFFFFFFF
% FFFFFFFFFFFFFFFFFFFF
%%EndPreview
%%EndProlog
%%Page: "one" 1
 4 4 moveto
 72 0 rlineto 0 16 rlineto -72 0 rlineto closepath
 8 setlinewidth stroke
%%Trailer
```

A.

Document Structuring Conventions (3.0)

New comments in version 3.0

All of the Document Structuring Conventions (DSC) comments are listed in alphabetic order, new version 3.0 comments are flagged with an asterisk(*).

```
%!PS-Adobe-3.0 * ß
%%?BeginFeatureQuery:          %%?EndFeatureQuery
%%?BeginFileQuery:             %%?EndFileQuery
%%?BeginFontListQuery:         %%?EndFontListQuery
%%?BeginFontQuery:             %%?EndFontQuery
%%?BeginPrinterQuery:          %%?EndPrinterQuery
%%?BeginProcSetQuery:          %%?EndProcSetQuery
%%?BeginQuery:                 %%?EndQuery
%%?BeginResourceQuery: *       %%?EndResourceQuery *
%%?BeginResourceListQuery: *   %%?EndResourceListQuery *
%%?BeginVMStatusQuery:         %%?EndVMStatusQuery
%%BeginBinary:                 %%EndBinary
%%BeginCustomColor:            %%EndCustomColor
%%BeginData: *                 %%EndData *
%%BeginDocument: ç             %%EndDocument ç
%%BeginEmulation: *            %%EndEmulation *
%%BeginExitServer:             %%EndExitServer
%%BeginFeature:                %%EndFeature
%%BeginFile:                   %%EndFile
%%BeginFont:                   %%EndFont
%%BeginObject:                 %%EndObject
%%BeginPageSetup:              %%EndPageSetup
%%BeginPaperSize:              %%EndPaperSize
%%BeginPreview: * ç            %%EndPreview * ç
%%BeginProcessColor:           %%EndProcessColor
%%BeginProcSet:                %%EndProcSet
%%BeginProlog: *               %%EndProlog
%%BeginResource: *             %%EndResource *
%%BeginSetup:                  %%EndSetup
```

```
%%BoundingBox: ß

%%CMYKCustomColor:
%%CreationDate: é
%%Creator: é

%%DocumentCustomColors:
%%DocumentFonts: ç
%%DocumentMedia: *
%%DocumentNeededFiles:
%%DocumentNeededFonts: ç
%%DocumentNeededProcSets:
%%DocumentNeededResources: * ç
%%DocumentPaperColors:
%%DocumentPaperForms:
%%DocumentPaperSizes:
%%DocumentPaperWeights:
%%DocumentPrinterRequired:
%%DocumentProcessColors:
%%DocumentProcSets:
%%DocumentSuppliedFiles:
%%DocumentSuppliedFonts:
%%DocumentSuppliedProcSets:
%%DocumentSuppliedResources: *

%%Emulations: *
%%EndComments
%%EOF
%%Extensions: * ç
%%For:

%%IncludeDocument: *
%%IncludeFeature: *
%%IncludeFile:
%%IncludeFont: ç
%%IncludeProcSet:
%%IncludeResource: * ç

%%LanguageLevel: * ç

%%OperatorIntervention: *
%%OperatorMessage: *
%%Orientation: *
```

```
%%Page:
%%PageBoundingBox:
%%PageCustomColors:
%%PageFonts:
%%PageFiles:
%%PageMedia: *
%%PageOrder: *
%%PageOrientation: *
%%PageProcessColors:
%%PageRequirements: *
%%PageResources: *
%%Pages:

%%PageTrailer:
%%PaperColor:
%%PaperForm:
%%PaperSize:
%%PaperWeight:
%%ProofMode:

%%Requirements:
%%RGBCustomColor:
%%Routing:

%%Title: é
%%Trailer:

%%VMlocation: *
%%VMusage: *
```

ß required in future EPSF version 3.0
ç conditionally required in future EPSF version 3.0
é recommended in future EPSF version 3.0

%%LanguageLevel: 2 means 'PostScript Level 2'.

The including application must surround the included EPS file by the *%%BeginDocument: -- %%EndDocument* comments.

BeginPreview: -- %%EndPreview comments must bracket an EPSI preview section.

The old *%%BeginBinary: -- %%EndBinary* comments will be substituted by *%%BeginData: -- %%EndData*.

The old *%%DocumentPaperColors:, %%DocumentPaperForms:, %%DocumentPaperSizes:, %%DocumentPaperWeights:* comments will be replaced by *%%DocumentMedia:*.

The old *%%PaperColor:, %%PaperForm:, %%PaperSize:, %%PaperWeight:* comments will be substituted by *%%PageMedia:*.

Resource management comments

Regarding the future EPSF specification, version 3.0, the requirement conventions and the new resource management comments are important.

The *%%DocumentFonts:* and *%%DocumentFiles:* comments may be discontinued in later versions of the DSC specification. The more general comments *%%DocumentNeededResources:* and *%%DocumentSuppliedResources:* will be used instead.

%%DocumentNeededResources:

```
%%DocumentNeededResources: <resources>
%%+ <resources>
```

This comment will provide a list of resources that are needed by the document, e.g. a font or a procedure set not contained within the document file. There should be at least one corresponding instance of the *%%IncludeResource:* comment for each resource listed by this comment.

Example:

```
%%DocumentNeededResources: font Times-Roman Sonata
%%+ font Helvetica-Bold
%%+ file UNILOGO EPS B
%%+ procset Adobe_Streamline_1.1 0 0
```

Note: As a general rule, different types of resources should be listed on separate lines using the *%%+* comment.

%%DocumentSuppliedResources:

```
%%DocumentSuppliedResources: <resources>
%%+ <resources>
```

This comment will list all of the resources that have been provided within the document print file. Specifically, there will be a *%%BeginResource: -- %%EndResource* pair for each resource in this list.

Example:

```
%!PS-Adobe-3.0
%%Creator: Adobe Illustrator 88(TM) 1.9.3
%%For: (TypeAlign)
%%Title: (Jupiter aligns)
%%CreationDate: (3/26/1990) (15:43)
%%DocumentSuppliedResources:
%%+ procset Adobe_Illustrator_1.1 0 0
%%BoundingBox: 17 48 431 224
%%EndComments
%%BeginResource: procset Adobe_Illustrator_1.1 0 0
 ...PostScript language code...
%%EndResource
%%EndProlog
 ...rest of the document...
%%EOF
```

It is assumed that all resources on the *%%DocumentSuppliedResources:* list are mutually exclusive of those resources found on the *%%DocumentNeededResources:* list.

Note: As a general rule, different types of resources should be listed on separate lines using the %%+ comment.

%%BeginResource: and %%EndResource

```
%%BeginResource: <resource> [<maxusage> <minusage>]
                        /* max VM used by resource */
                        /* min VM used by resource */
```

These comments delimit a resource that is defined by PostScript language code directly in the document file (e.g. downloadable fonts). Resources may be for instance fonts, files, or procedure sets (procset).

The *%%Begin(End)ProcSet:, %%Begin(End)File:* and *%%Begin(End)Font:* comments may be discontinued in later versions of the DSC specification. The more general comments *%%BeginResource:* and *%%EndResource* will be used instead.

%%IncludeResource:

```
%%IncludeResource: <resource>
```

Indicates that the named resource must be included at this point in the document by the print manager. The resource name specified also should appear in the *%%Document-NeededResources:* list.

Example:

```
%!PS-Adobe-3.0
%%Creator: Micrografx Designer
%%For: (PC Info Center) (Uni Zurich)
%%Title: (Fendant.art)
%%CreationDate: (7/25/90) (8:25 am)
%%DocumentNeededResources: procset MGXPS_2.1 0 0
%%+ font ZapfDingbats Korinna-Regular
%%EndComments
%%IncludeResource: procset MGXPS_2.1 0 0
%%IncludeResource: font ZapfDingbats
%%IncludeResource: font Korinna-Regular
%%EndProlog
 ...rest of the document...
%%EOF
```

The *%%IncludeProcSet:*, *%%IncludeFile:* and *%%IncludeFont:* comments may be discontinued in later versions of the DSC specification. The more general *%%IncludeResource:* comment will be used instead.

Document Structuring Conventions comment summary

This summary is contained in [4]. There are

General conventions   Header comments, e.g. *%%BoundingBox:*, *%%EndComments*, *%%EndProlog*. Body comments, e.g. *%%Begin(End)Data:*, *%%Trailer*. And page comments.

Requirement conventions

Header comments, e.g. *%%DocumentNeededResources:*, *%%DocumentSuppliedResources:*. Body comments, e.g. *%%Begin(End)Resource:*, *%%IncludeResource:*. And page comments.

Color separation conventions

Header comments, e.g. *%%CMYKCustomColor:*. Body comments and page comments.

Query conventions   E.g. *%!PS-Adobe-3.0 Query*.

B.

EPSF Screen Representations

Page without EPSF

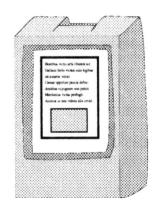

Page with EPSF
without Preview

Page with EPSF
with Preview

Page with EPSF
with Display PostScript

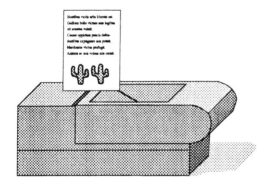

C.

Bibliography

1. Adobe Systems Inc. (1986), *PostScript Language, Tutorial and Cookbook* (blue book), Addison-Wesley.

2. Adobe Systems Inc. (1990), *PostScript Language, Reference Manual* (red book), Addison-Wesley.

3. Adobe Systems Inc. (1988), *PostScript Language, Program Design* (File Interchange Standards), Addison-Wesley.

4. Adobe Systems Inc. (1990), *Document Structuring Conventions Specification, version 3.0*, Mountain View.

5. Adobe Systems Inc. (1988), *Cooperative Printing, Guidelines for a distributed printing environment*, Mountain View.

6. Adobe Systems Inc. (1987), *PostScript Printer Description File Specification*, Mountain V.

7. Adobe Systems Inc. (1987), *Adobe Illustrator Document Specifications*, Mountain View.

8. Adobe Systems Inc. (1988), *Display PostScript, Perspective for Software Developers*, Mountain View.

9. Adobe Systems Inc. (1988), *Display PostScript, Client Library Reference Manual*, Mountain View.

10. Adobe Systems Inc. (1988), *PostScript Language, Extensions for the Display PostScript System*, Mountain View.

11. Adobe Systems Inc. (1988), *PostScript Language, Color Extensions,* Mountain View.

12. Braswell, Frank M. (1989), *Inside PostScript,* Peachpit Press, Berkeley CA.

13. Holzgang, David A. (1988), *Understanding PostScript Programming,* Sybex, San Francisco.

14. Holzgang, David A. (1988), *Mastering Adobe Illustrator,* Sybex, San Francisco.

15. Pipeline Associates, Inc. (1990), *The PostScript Language Journal,* 239 Main Street, West Orange, NJ 07052.

16. Roth, Stephen F. (1988), *Real World PostScript* (Writing Device-Independent PostScript), Addison-Wesley.

17. Vollenweider, Peter (1988), *PostScript − Konzeption, Anwendung, Mischen von Text und Grafik,* Carl Hanser, München.

18. Webster, Bruce F. (1989), *The NeXT Book,* Addison-Wesley.

Index

$42.00

4-25-92